Madame Clairevoyant's
GUIDE TO THE STARS

Madame Clairevoyant's

GUIDE
TO THE
STARS

Astrology, Our Icons, and Our Selves

CLAIRE COMSTOCK-GAY

HARPER

An Imprint of HarperCollins*Publishers*

HarperCollins books may be purchased for educational, business, or sales promotional use. For information, please email the Special Markets Department at SPsales@harpercollins.com.

FIRST EDITION

Designed by Bonni Leon-Berman

Library of Congress Cataloging-in-Publication Data has been applied for.

ISBN 978-0-06-291333-3

20 21 22 23 24   LSC   10 9 8 7 6 5 4 3 2 1

*C*ontents

Madame Clairevoyant's

GUIDE TO THE STARS

Introduction

SOME YEARS AGO YOU WERE BORN SOMEWHERE ON PLANET EARTH. You took your first breath and became a person with a body of your own—no longer existing inside your parent, no longer existing only in the future, but a full and distinct being, with your own needs, your own hunger, your own heart pumping your own blood through you. And this moment of brand-new personhood was the moment, astrologically speaking, that formed you: the broad outlines of your personality, the landscape of your heart, the challenges and desires and unthinkably miraculous gifts that would be yours as you move through the days and years of your life.

Though the possible uses for astrology are vast and varied—from planning a garden to predicting political unrest; from diagnosing illness to scheduling weddings—it shines brightest in our modern world not as a tool for deciphering omens and curses or foretelling our predestined lives and deaths, but as a mirror to our inner world. In a world with advanced satellite technology and cutting-edge medicine, astrology still offers something science cannot (although it may try): a sharp, wise, nuanced system for understanding ourselves and our messy lives and our mysterious, tangled-up feelings.

This is what many of us arrive at astrology in search of: a way to understand why we're *like* this. Why are we so loud and so frustrating, or so hard to satisfy, or so desperate for reassurance or attention or praise? Why can't we seem to just act normal, get our lives together, sand down the spikier parts of our personalities? Why can't we manage to just force ourselves to be simple, to make our lives and our personalities small and clear and just like everybody else's?

Astrology's skeptics and detractors like to make a fuss about how foolish it is to imagine that, simply by looking to the stars, we can know what the future will bring. But to argue this is to completely misunderstand one of modern astrology's central purposes—not to find our destinies, but to find our actually existing, living human selves.

AND STILL, FOR MANY YEARS, I dismissed astrology, too, not out of reasoned intellectual conviction but simply because it showed me nothing about myself I could recognize. I was about eleven when I learned that my sign was Sagittarius, the archer, sign of intellect and adventure and, as the books would have it, athleticism. To my preteen self, this was laughable in its wrongness. I was an awkward moper, a quiet dreamer, a comically bad athlete. My greatest athletic achievement was when I pitched a winning softball game because nobody on the other team could process that my pitches were really *that slow*. I was entirely too confused by the world to be, as the list of my apparent traits told me I was, "spontaneous." Quietness, loneliness, strangeness—these were the qualities that felt foundational to who I was. The cheery, carefree Sagittarius the astrology books described was another person entirely.

So I shrugged off my supposedly identity-defining sun sign, and—because I had no idea that there was anything more to it—astrology in general. It took nearly a decade for me to reconsider. During that time, I looked for myself in literature and sad indie rock and unfulfilled teenage horniness. I looked for myself in the poetry shelves of the library and in queer punk shows and feminist zine fests, in friendships and relationships and sessions with an exceedingly gentle therapist who didn't understand me at all. I kept learning so much about the world, but none of it could explain to me why I was like this: so quiet but so restless, so full of hunger but so afraid of expressing my desires.

When I graduated from college and moved to New York, I was surprised when I found myself surrounded by people as critical and curious and distrustful of authority as I was and who nonetheless talked about astrology like it was interesting and useful. At a party in a Brooklyn backyard, I joked to a woman who brought up astrology that it couldn't be real, for I was really no kind of Sagittarius at all. "Ohhh," she said, smiling, "but what's your rising sign?" This was the first I'd ever heard of rising signs. Before that moment I had a vague idea that there existed such a thing as an "astrological chart," but it had still never quite occurred to me that astrology was, for practical purposes, anything more than horoscopes in the newspaper or cheesy books for teens at the local chain bookstore. It hadn't occurred to me until then that my own astrological chart was something I could access and that it might show me a picture of myself that was much clearer, truer, and more interesting than the unrealistic Sagittarius descriptions I had read before.

After the party that night, I opened my laptop and typed my date, time, and place of birth into an online birth chart calculator, and it told me my rising sign was Cancer. Cancer rising, I read on the website, can be sensitive, vulnerable, generous, and dreamy, but also moody, avoidant, secretive, and lazy. The sharp, specific correctness of it hurt my feelings. But more than that, it filled me with relief that someone finally saw me clearly—that someone was finally telling me the truth about myself.

This moment of bracing recognition was enough to change my entire relationship to astrology. What I saw there became my gateway, my door, my Rosetta stone: the key that let me interpret the rest of my chart. With this one piece of information locked into place, suddenly the rest of astrology's potential snapped into focus, too. I could return to Sagittarius with new eyes and see in myself the Sagittarian elements I'd missed before: expansive curiosity, generous idealism, a lack of attention to detail, a need for freedom. And although I didn't know what else it all meant yet, I could see that I had an entire chart full of planets, full of placements, full of secrets and mysteries about myself that I could now learn to unlock.

It was only at this point that I could begin to access what astrology really had to offer me. In my own life, I didn't need it as a predictor of the future, or as a guide to practical matters, or even as a quick way to determine potential compatibility with a crush. What I *did* need, and hadn't found anywhere else—not from my good and loving parents, not from my rich and fulfilling friendships, not from therapy or literature or exercise or long hours spent trying to figure out my own brain—was an affirmation that the way I was wired was fundamentally okay.

After so much time spent imagining that there was, ultimately, a single best way to be a person—one that we all, to greater or lesser degrees, continually fail to attain—astrology invited me to radically re-envision the world. It showed me a world where people can act and feel and desire in different and sometimes diametrically opposed ways, but none of these ways are fundamentally bad. None, for that matter, are fundamentally *good*, either, but all are equally valid ways of being a person, and equally necessary in our broad, rich universe.

Astrology gave me the understanding that all the troublesome Cancer rising traits that I couldn't for the life of me get rid of weren't signs of some kind of damage to be repaired but, rather, natural if sometimes inconvenient features of my inner landscape. The problem wasn't that I had a defective personality, only that I kept trying to twist my personality into something other than what it was. I had been trying to rebuild my whole self in a new shape when all I really needed to do was learn how to use what I'd been given, how to live as me.

I had once thought of astrology as a system for shoving our wild, unmanageable selves into broad and simplistic categories—a system for circumventing the difficulties of the full, complex, contradictory realities of living a human life. But what I saw then, at that moment, was that astrology offered just the opposite: a space to explore complexity, to explain contradiction, to see the beauty and sense of being exactly the people we are.

FOR MOST PEOPLE, THE INITIAL point of entry into astrology is the discovery of their sun sign; that was true in my case as well. It's the easiest place to start, by a wide margin: all you need to know is the day you were born. From there, astrology can stay as simple or become as complex as you need or want it to be. But at all levels, in all incarnations, astrology is based on the idea that our small, earthbound selves are inextricably linked with the stars and planets in our sky. "As above, so below," goes astrology's foundational axiom: by some strange and unknown force, each one of us is intimately connected to the cosmos, and you can find a personal map of these connections in your birth chart.

At its most basic, your birth chart deals in combinations of planets and signs. Each one of the astrological planets—from Mercury to Pluto, plus the sun and moon—can be found in your chart, and each one exerts a pull over a specific area of your life on earth. The sun and the moon hold the strongest influence over our daily lives and personalities, and they'll be the ones discussed most in this book. The sun, with its massive gravitational pull, governs the orbit of the rest of the planets in the sky, and it can also be thought of as the force directing the rest of the planetary placements in your chart. It's the sun sign that shapes your personality most broadly— and the one that indicates your truest purpose in life.

While your sun sign reflects the way you engage with the world around you, your moon sign shows how you engage with your inner world. Just as the moon guides the daily ebb and flow of the tides, it also guides the daily ebb and flow of your moods and feelings. Close to earth and yet still mysterious, it shapes your deepest emotional core, your emotional baggage, your instinctive responses and reactions. After the sun, it's one of the most important placements in a chart and one of the most important indicators of who you are.

Even if you aren't well versed in astrology, you probably already have an intuitive familiarity with some of the planets and what they stand for. You could probably guess that Mars, for instance—the red planet, the god of war, the planet from which men supposedly come—shapes your animal urges, drive, and aggression; or that Venus, culturally coded as feminine, shapes the ways you experience and express sensuality and love; or that Mercury—named for the Roman messenger god—is the planet of communication and thought.

As they move along their orbits, the planets pass through the twelve sections of the sky associated with each one of the twelve zodiac signs. Each sign, from Aries to Pisces, represents a set of unique qualities and characteristics; while a planet moves through that sign's segment of sky, it takes on that sign's traits. So if Mars was in Aries (confident, brash) when you were born, you'll express aggression differently than you would if Mars had been in Taurus (stubborn, determined). If Venus was in Gemini (curious, adaptable), you'll seek out a different kind of love than you would if it had been in Cancer (sensitive, nurturing). The planets and the signs don't act on us in isolation. They combine and react; they activate each other's powers. There's no way to feel a "pure" Virgo energy; we can only feel Virgo's energy as it is embodied and mediated through the movement of the planets.

It gets complicated quickly—sometimes in ways that feel thrilling and illuminating, other times feeling more like a particularly unrewarding page of math homework. Astrology is packed with simultaneously moving parts, and this is just the beginning. In addition to the twelve signs, for instance, there are also twelve astrological houses, which determine the domain—work, family, love relationships, health—where these planetary influences are likely to appear. Just like planetary placements, the houses are positioned differently for

everyone. The houses are much less straightforward than planetary placements: there are multiple systems that can be used
to calculate the houses, and they cannot be calculated without
knowing your precise time of birth. For the most part, this
book won't deal with house placements, with one important
exception: the beginning edge of your first house, also known
as your rising sign, or ascendant.

The rising sign is, along with the sun and moon, one of the
so-called big three signs that we all possess, the primary indicators of your overall personality and self. Your rising sign
represents the public face you show to the world, or the way
others immediately perceive you, or the way that you strive
to be seen. For some people, a rising sign can operate like a
mask covering the "true" self; for others, it's more like another, equally true aspect of the self. Sometimes a rising sign
feels more intuitively, immediately true to who you are than
your sun sign. My own rising sign in Cancer—dreamy but unrealistic, generous but touchy and evasive—was initially easier for me to understand than my sun sign; even now, my
Sagittarian bluntness and independence can come as a shock
to people who expect nothing else beneath the soft-spoken,
loving Cancer public face they know me to be.

The main point to take away is that your sun sign—the
one you'd read about in a magazine horoscope, or that you'd
name if someone asked for your sign—isn't your *only* sign; it's
not the only energy astrology allows you to claim. If you've
ever felt that your sun sign is inaccurate or reductive—that

it doesn't tell the whole story of who you are—that's because it doesn't, and was never really intended to. The influence of the other planets might be stranger, more oblique, more difficult to see, but it's there, from nearby Mars to faraway Pluto. Although there are only twelve zodiac signs, there are 144 possible combinations of sun and moon, and 1,728 possible sun/moon/rising combinations. After factoring in the other planets—not to mention the houses, other placements like asteroids, planetoids, and nodes—a birth chart has space for nearly limitless possibilities and contradictions and puzzles and surprises.

What this makes so clear is that astrology's job isn't to categorize us or to shove us into one of twelve pigeonholes and keep us there for life. The purpose of the twelve zodiac categories isn't to contain us or to absolve us of the need to grow or change as people. Rather, it's to help us delve into our weirdest, best, most thorny contradictions—not in order to flatten them out but to give us a language for the wild abundance of our real, confusing selves.

SOMETIMES THE OTHER PLACEMENTS IN your chart can strengthen and amplify the pull of your sun sign; I have three additional planets in Sagittarius, for instance. At other times they'll complicate, deepen, or contradict the story your sun sign tells about you; for me, Mercury and Mars in Scorpio bring a note of darkness, of intensity, of depth, to a chart otherwise filled with Sagittarian optimism and expansiveness. At other times still, a planet's influence can remain mysterious to us, even vexing. My moon sign—the sign of instincts, emotions, and our deepest inner needs—is in Capricorn, and it's hard to reconcile what I know about this placement (desirous of security, respectful of authority, rigorous and controlled) with what I know, or think I know, about my restless, disorganized, insubordinate self.

But in astrology, there's no picking and choosing. It asks us to accept that there are cosmic forces far bigger than we are and over which we have no control. Unlike with many other personality assessments, if you know when and where you were born, there's no chance of getting a false readout on your birth chart—no room to wonder whether you interpreted quiz questions incorrectly, no way to game the system by answering in a way you know will lead to the results you want, no chance to tell yourself that on a different day, in a different mood, you'd be sorted into a different category. Astrology is based on unchangeable and irrefutable physical facts. If the moon was in Capricorn when I was born, then the moon was in Capricorn, whether I like it or not; there's no way to wriggle out of it.

Beneath this apparent prescriptivism, however, astrology opens out into a vast and beautiful space of interpretation and movement. The positions of the planets may already be determined for you, and there may be fundamental qualities about ourselves that we'll never be able to change or erase, but the *meanings* of the signs and planets—the ways we'll *live* with the selves we were born into—are constantly being navigated and negotiated, interpreted and reinterpreted. This is the fundamental tension astrology rests on: our deepest selves have already been determined by forces bigger than us, but it's still up to us to continually interpret the pieces we're made of, to continually make meaning of the lives we've been given.

In my case, for instance, being unable to reject or escape my Capricorn moon has created space for me to be honest about the ways I contradict myself, the ways my own heart can be mysterious even to me, the ways my needs and desires jumble and crash up against one another. My favorite way to see myself is as a person who is, in a quiet and unflashy way, completely unafraid of change. And this is a true way of seeing myself, as my history of quitting jobs and ending relationships and recklessly moving between cities indicates. Yet the unavoidable fact of my Capricorn moon requires me to acknowledge another, equally real part of me that *does* want security, that wants to be useful, that wants to live not sloppily but *right*.

An astrological chart holds space for you to want more than one thing at once, to *be* more than one thing at once. The desire for stability threaded through my desire for freedom and change doesn't make me a failed or defective Sagittarius. It just makes me human. At its best, astrology gives us tools for understanding ourselves and other people without measuring ourselves against some unattainable, one-size-fits-all idea of how a person should be. Instead astrology lets us see ourselves as ourselves—and other people as their own strange and complicated selves, too.

ASTROLOGY HAS NOT, OF COURSE, always been used as a tool for introspection. In ancient Babylon, where astrology originated in the second millennium BCE, it wasn't used to find insight into individuals' lives or personalities but rather to understand and predict events in the world. The stars and planets were understood to offer omens and messages that could be used to maintain a ruler's power, to predict weather, to provide insights into the best times for planting and harvesting crops. As it spread through the ancient world, it was practiced by scholars and clerics and monks—and even, in the medieval world, by physicians. Like any body of knowledge, though, astrology grew and changed and developed, and new astronomical concepts began to challenge astrology's claim to scientific truth. Heliocentrism, in particular, undermined astrology's practice of treating the sun as just another planet—although the most powerful one—revolving around the earth. And as astronomy's authority expanded, astrology was demoted to "pseudoscience"—or, more tactfully, "something other than science."

In spite of this, astrology and its influence didn't disappear; its trajectory is strikingly different from, say, alchemy. What it did, instead, was adapt and proliferate. While serious astrologers continued to study and practice outside the main-stream, *inside* the mainstream, astrology was recast as some-thing popular, accessible, and vaguely silly—particularly after British astrologer R. H. Naylor began publishing the first newspaper horoscopes in the 1930s. Relieved of its official institutional power (Nancy Reagan and her astrologer Joan Quigley notwithstanding), astrology was able to fill a new need. For while advancing scientific knowledge offered other, more verifiable ways of understanding weather or crop sea-sons or politics, our private inner worlds and our messy, com-plicated relationships with each other remained wild and mysterious, never fully explainable by science. And in this role astrology continues to thrive, accessible and anarchic, out-side the halls of the academy, outside of our Enlightenment inheritance of logic and rationality.

Regardless of its current popularity, there is still a resound-ing lack of peer-reviewed evidence that astrology is "real." When I first began learning about it, I found countless articles attempting to persuade readers of astrology's nonscientific and disreputable nature, citing instances where astrology di-verges from the astronomical reality of the sky, or referring to experiments that failed to find any evidence that astrol-ogy might "work," or pointing to astrological predictions that turned out to be famously, massively wrong.

But this kind of thinking seems, at least to me, to miss the point. Trying to determine modern astrology's accuracy or relevance with a scientific experiment seems nearly as unhelpful as it would be to use an experiment to determine the accuracy of Aretha Franklin's voice, or the correctness of Pablo Neruda's love poems, or the scientific validity of Yoko Ono's conceptual performances. It's possible to interpret and critique all of these things; it's possible to love them or hate them; it's possible for them to rise and fall and disappear from our cultural consciousness, but science can't tell you whether they're "right" or not. There's a science to astrology, but to understand it, to read it—to *use* it for anything at all—relies on our imperfect and human interpretive powers.

Astrology's tenacious refusal to disappear, to shrink before the dictates of our dominant modes of knowledge, is also, I truly believe, its own kind of magic. It offers us a chance to know ourselves according to a different set of rules than what's currently acceptable in the realm of science. Astrology offers us a chance to see ourselves and all the ways we're too sensitive or noisy or ambitious, too sad or insecure or confrontational or rebellious. It gives us an interpretive model still largely unbound by rules of correctness or good taste, or by its own respectability. Astrology doesn't know you better than you know yourself, but it might open the door into the more challenging rooms in your heart. How wonderful it is to be allowed this space that defies all our ideas about respectability in favor of a different kind of love—openhearted, potentially corny, potentially wrong!

After all, modern astrology has never really been about studying the planets or the sky. They aren't our objects but our mirrors. The cosmic world reflects the human world, and the human world reflects the cosmos. Astrology encourages us to see ourselves not as isolated observers but as beings inextricably linked to the workings of the universe—as vast, as complicated, as beautiful and wild as the stars. For all its basis in the cosmos, astrology's best gift to us is to serve as a tool for understanding what it is to be a person. The planets themselves may be physical facts, but our understanding of them can never be anything but human. The planets can only tell us what we're willing to see; depending on our perspective from down here on earth, their messages to us can be limiting or liberating, restrictive or radical.

Ultimately, astrology can only be as wise and as generous as we are. The signs and their meanings are constantly changing and evolving, just as humans keep changing, just as the world keeps changing. An astrological chart might be celestially, mathematically pure, but our interpretations of that chart will always be human, limited by the things we can know and feel, by our particular life experiences, by the cultures we live in. Nobody—not even the wisest or most rigorous or most intuitive astrologer—has a direct line to the meaning of the sky. We're all looking up from here on earth, doing our best to interpret what we see.

These interpretations will always be informed by our own consciousnesses, and limited by the same mental and material constraints that limit our everyday lives. The cultures we live in produce the lenses we use to look at the universe; the stories and jokes and gossip we grow up with determine the stories we learn how to tell. Even in astrology's nonnormative world, cultural norms, gender roles, and white supremacy still shape the ways we're able to see. Aries, for instance, is understood to be a "bold" sign, but how do we know what boldness really looks like? If you're not paying close attention, only the loudest, most brazen types of boldness even register as bold at all.

Astrology offers one way to practice seeing the types of Aries boldness, for example, that have been suppressed and ignored. It offers a fresh set of interpretive tools, a structured method for observing the world with curious, generous eyes, and for seeing ourselves and each other with clarity. But for this to happen, looking at the sky isn't enough; it's necessary to look around here on earth as well.

This book will look for evidence of each sign's energy in the lives and creative output of real-life public figures: writers, musicians, actors, artists, thinkers. This book focuses primarily on the sun signs of its subjects not as an endpoint but as a beginning, an entryway into astrological thinking. The point isn't to gain insight into the lives of famous people but rather to show how they animate their sign's energy, and to show how we might learn to find these energies in ourselves and each other.

My aim is not simply to explain the energies of the twelve signs—not to provide a reference book or study guide—but to offer ways of seeing, ways of noticing, ways of imagining. On offer here are structuring, animating stories that can make the details, the contradictions, the energies we're all made of, come alive. To this end it's a book designed for reading *all* the signs, not just your own sun sign. If you want to know, ultimately, why you are the way you are—why you're like *this* and not like *that*—your sun sign alone won't give you what you're really looking for. Every one of the signs moves around you and through you. You interact with every one of the signs every day; every person you encounter is made of a complex mixture of astrological energies. The better you can learn to see each one, the wiser, more generous, more intuitive you'll become.

Expanding our emotional vocabularies can seem like a frivolous undertaking right now, when oceans are rising and forests are burning and the most powerful people in the world seem hell-bent on making this planet unlivable for the rest of us. And it is, in some ways, slight: getting right with our feelings won't be enough to save us. But asserting the value of our wild, multitudinous feelings is not unserious work. This is the work of acknowledging our enduring humanity; it's the work of continuing to love and hold each other even in an unpredictable world. This is the work of learning (if we can manage it) to love each other *better* than we ever did before. Astrology is an analytical language, but it's an imaginative, emotional language, too. It's a tool for seeing and loving the world, other people, and ourselves. This guide is a way of seeing.

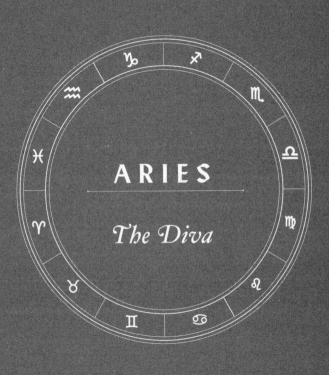

ARIES

The Diva

IN DECEMBER 1997, JAMES CAMERON, A LEO, RELEASED A MOVIE. Celine Dion, an Aries, released a song.

The movie was *Titanic* and the song was the soaring, ubiquitous "My Heart Will Go On."

I had just turned ten, and while I was emphatically not allowed to go to the theater to see a PG-13 movie, Dion's song poured out of speakers all over town. In my fifth-grade classroom, out at recess, and on the bus after school, the kids lucky enough to have parents who had let them see the movie would re-create the best bits for the rest of us.

"I'll never let go, Jack," they'd gasp before sliding tragically to the bottom of a snowbank.

As someone uninitiated, Dion's song was the only clue I had into the movie's grand drama. The story this song told me was that this passion was so straightforward, so pure, so unabashed, that it became embarrassing—a comedy routine for a band of rowdy children.

Celine Dion, however, wasn't the least bit embarrassed. At the 1998 Academy Awards, she performed "My Heart Will Go On" in a long, dark blue turtleneck dress and a monster of a diamond necklace. (In *Billboard*'s 2017 "oral history" of the song, Dion said she insisted on the turtleneck: "Everybody goes for chiffon dresses and décolletage, and I really wanted a turtleneck dress. [Michael Kors] said, 'A turtleneck?!' Yes. Long-sleeve. Very tight. Just navy blue, like the water, but very deep down, like the ocean.")

While fog spilled across the blue-lit stage behind her, Dion stood almost entirely still as she sang, her feet planted, not dancing or walking or even swaying to the music. But as the song built, she began to stretch out her arms, reaching toward something above or outside of her body. In the song's famous key change—glorious, or maudlin, or both—she pounded her chest with one fist, a nonsense gesture, a gesture of pure feeling.

This is what her fans love about her, and what drives her haters to distraction: a fire too big to be politely contained by the limits of her body. A feeling too big to stay inside the lines.

CELINE DION IS AN ARIES. And the things people love and hate in equal parts about her are also the things we love and hate about Aries more generally: a fearless willingness to follow where passion leads. A bright, pure will too powerful to be held back. A joyful, fiery confidence that can and will break all the rules of decorum. A bold straightforwardness that makes it possible to live courageously, following one's own deep needs and desires even when they run counter to all social norms. All of this unapologetic vitality and drive can sometimes strike others as tasteless, annoying, even rude. And for people who do feel tightly constrained by social rules, to people constantly asked to sacrifice their own needs and happiness for the sake of some larger group, Aries's bold freedom can inspire a feeling that looks like irritation but that in reality might cover up a deeper and truer feeling: envy.

Even mediated through the radio, her voice piped onto a noisy bus full of elementary schoolers back in 1997, Dion transmitted her Aries energy directly to our brains: not one of us seemed able to sing the chorus without clutching a hand to our heart, or flinging an arm in the air, or even, for the particularly bold among us, getting down on one knee. I can't know for sure, but I don't think that any of us schoolchildren were allowed—or, for that matter, wanted—to stay up late to watch her chest-pounding Academy Awards performance. So it follows that we weren't mimicking it. Instead, even as we clowned, we were recognizing some of that Aries buoyance, and feeling it, and matching it with our own bodies.

ARIES IS THE FIRST SIGN of the zodiac year, which begins not on January first but rather in the spring, around the time of the vernal equinox. Located at the year's fresh beginning, Aries is often understood to be the newborn of the zodiac, filled with pure instinct and a sweet springtime clarity, as when the world seems to finally, instantly, turn green again. Just as the birds return and trees put out buds, seemingly without planning or thought, there's something intuitive about Aries energy, too. It's an energy born not of deliberation but of pure, natural instinct and the sheer joy in being alive.

Because Aries wisdom isn't complicated or conflicted, it

can be fearless. Or maybe it works the other way: because Aries wisdom is fearless, it is able to be uncomplicated. An Aries can experience desires that are vast and ambitious without tying herself up in knots of doubt and insecurity. She simply moves forward and get things started. Aries energy can therefore often be impatient, confident in its desires and unwilling to wait. Like fellow fire sign Leo, Aries can bring whole new worlds into being, but where Leo often accomplishes this by leading and directing other people, Aries's power comes from its own personal strength of will.

Strength of will is not, in reality, a gendered trait, but our understanding of Aries's strong will often does slide into gendered terms. Aries is ruled by Mars, the red planet, the god of war; it shares a name with Mars's Greek counterpart, Ares. These associations can haunt our understanding of what Aries is all about; the muscled, classical warrior with helmet and spear may feel emblematic. In turn, this masculine warrior figure can blur and bleed into our understanding of Aries's raw, assertive confidence; straightforward power and strength, then, become cast in our minds as tools best suited for war and conflict, weapons wielded by men.

And while this is not entirely false or unhelpful, it's also not the only way—or even the best way—to understand what this kind of energy can do. The classical warrior Ares is one kind of real Aries, yes, but there is another Aries in a tight dress; there's an Aries with eyeliner and an updo; there's an Aries belting it out at the microphone in front of a full orchestra. What could we learn about Aries, and courage, and power, by looking not just to the warrior but to the diva?

The two might not ultimately be so far apart. Warrior and diva converge in many of the less-than-favorable reviews of Celine Dion's music: *The New* Rolling Stone *Album Guide*, for instance, calls her voice "a club with which to bonk listeners." In this formulation, her voice is both instrument and weapon, her assertive musical energy a kind of attack. Music that makes you feel with such intensity that you have no choice but to move your own body to meet it—a hand on a heart, an arm outstretched—can feel like a gift if you want it, but if you don't, it can feel like an invading force.

In this review, *Rolling Stone* goes on to warn readers that Dion's diva energy is not isolated to her but is in fact symptomatic of a bigger pattern, symbolic of a particular strain in pop music where bigger is better and where thoughtfulness and good taste fall to the wayside in favor of something more brash, bright, and instinctual. This is visible in a long line of artistic kinship, where Dion is the endpoint to a "chain of drastic devolution that goes Aretha-Whitney-Mariah." And in this lineage, Celine Dion, Aretha Franklin, and Mariah Carey all have their sun sign in Aries. (Carey has Mercury and Venus in Aries, too.) Although Whitney Houston's sun sign is Leo, her moon—the sign ruling over her instincts, her reactions, her emotional world—is in Aries.

This matters not because I think astrology gave these musicians their voices, and not because I think knowing they have Aries sun signs can shed light on who they really are, but because it can help us to understand how we look at them. It can help us explain why we tell the stories we do about famous singers, and indeed ourselves.

ARIES IS A FIRE SIGN; these signs are generally understood to be spontaneous and energetic and creative. They can be intense, in ways that sometimes feel good and sometimes feel bad. While the idea of "fieriness" conjures up traits like ferocity and danger, there's more to it than this. It's useful to think of fire not only as something that can rage, destructive, through cities and forests but also as something that can keep a house warm, as something that can light the way forward through a dark space.

Listen for the bright Aries current running through Aretha Franklin's most iconic hit, "Respect." She didn't write the song; that was Otis Redding, a Virgo, who released his own recording two years earlier in 1965. But in Aretha Franklin's hands, the song becomes something entirely different from Redding's song of a downtrodden, hardworking breadwinner who just wants his woman to show him some respect when he comes home. Under the power of Franklin's Aries fire, it becomes a song about a different kind of love: one that isn't unearned or unconditional but that nonetheless is easily, joyfully given. There's no wheedling here, no begging, no cajoling. While there's a thrill in the chase, maybe, a bright joy in the pursuit of love, there's no satisfaction in games or deceit. "I ain't gonna do you wrong while you're gone," Franklin sings. "Ain't gonna do you wrong 'cause I don't wanna": Aries believes too much in the possibility of sweetness up ahead to expend energy on cheating or trickery or revenge.

The heart of Franklin's bargain—and the core of Aries love—is that an Aries will love fully and freely and honestly, but only if they are loved as fully, freely, and honestly in return. Otherwise, Franklin sings, you might walk in and find out I'm gone. This isn't mournful or resentful, nor is it quite a threat. It's just the truth of the matter.

It would be a mistake to imagine the Aries straightforwardness to be only a mark of conflict or aggression. There's more joy here than that. Franklin's narrator in "Respect" is a person starry-eyed with belief in herself and her options in this world. She is a person unwilling to agree to an unbearable bargain, an unlivable picture of love. Listen to the ecstatic, driving "Sock it to me, sock it to me, sock it to me." Listen to the exuberance and rhythm and clarity in Franklin's classic chant: "R-E-S-P-E-C-T / Find out what it means to me / R-E-S-P-E-C-T . . ." Listening to her sing her desires into being, you could almost start to believe that your own desire for respect and love doesn't have to be so complicated, either, and that this desire doesn't have to be a burden at all but rather a joyful and life-giving force. You could almost start to believe what Aries keeps trying to show us: there's no shame in believing you deserve a life that's not just survivable but magnificent.

Along with Cancer, Libra, and Capricorn, Aries is a cardinal sign, one that marks the start of a new season; Aries marks the beginning of spring. Cardinal signs are filled with leadership and drive. Cardinal signs start projects without knowing if they'll finish, trusting instead that some momentum or courage or skill will be enough to carry them through. They aren't afraid of beginnings or the work to come. When an Aries leaps ahead into an unknown space, it's not out of fear of the thing behind them but out of desire for the thing up ahead.

Mariah Carey's classic "All I Want for Christmas Is You," released in 1994 but still dominant on the charts more than twenty years later, is in some ways a throwback, incorporating musical influences from the forties, fifties, and sixties with its jubilant layers of church bells, sleigh bells, and bright piano harmonies. But in other ways this song was something completely new: a star at the top of her game, coming off the career high of her 1993 album *Music Box*, deciding next to make a Christmas record. According to Carey's cowriter Walter Afanasieff, there was some question of whether this was a good move. Carey did it anyway. Afanasieff questioned the direction Carey wanted to take the vocals: he thought they sounded silly, like a singer practicing scales. Carey did it anyway. Decades later, Carey's voice sails out of speakers all across

America every year at Christmastime. Her vocals are clear and unwavering, climbing higher and higher. It's essentially the only contemporary addition to the Christmas canon. Mariah Carey, an Aries, did that.

Sometimes this cardinal sign energy means an Aries can be impatient, unwilling to wait for permission to act. At its bright best, Aries energy is pure and alive and unstoppable. Beneath anxiety, beneath doubt, beneath thought, there's a space where muscle and spirit and force of will take over; this is the Aries gift. If an Aries seems to sometimes carry a current of aggression, it's matched by a twin current of desire, of pure confidence, of absolute sweetness. You can hear both moods braided together in Carey's "Always Be My Baby." Ostensibly a song about a breakup, the mood is one of optimism, not sorrow or self-doubt, "'cause I know in my heart babe / Our love will never die." Carey sings that her lover "can't escape" her with such purity in her voice, it's almost enough to forget how unnerving the words could sound spoken by someone else; the propulsive optimism of Carey's voice is enough to carry you away.

Mariah Carey's sure, assertive sweetness marks the Aries energy at its best, but no sign's magic comes without a corresponding strangeness or darkness or sorrow. Along with Aries's bright power come the seeds for selfishness and prickliness—the potential, in the joyful pursuit of their own wild plans and desires, to trample someone else. Aries stereotypes would have you believe it's the sign of selfish hotheads, the sign of reckless and insensitive people too caught up in their own ambitions to act with real kindness or care.

There's something about this that people love to watch. There's a certain glee that creeps into their voices when they talk about Aretha Franklin's famous "feuds"—with Dionne Warwick or Roberta Flack or Natalie Cole or Diana Ross or Gladys Knight or Tina Turner or Beyoncé—or the rude and selfish way she's said to have treated her sisters Erma and Carolyn, also singers. She once fired Al Green! In 2015 she snapped photos on her cell phone through the entire first act of *The Color Purple*! "Aretha Franklin Is a Worse Person Than You Thought," the Page Six headline happily announced.

There's a similar glee in the internet's endless echoing, through image and video and GIF, of Mariah Carey's answer to the journalist who asked what she thought about fellow musician Jennifer Lopez: a bright-eyed smile, a shake of her head, and her devastating one-line answer: "I don't know her." Later, Carey would insist that she had spoken from a genuine place of not knowing. Whether or not this is true, the moment became an emblem of the kind of triumphant rudeness that we'd watch her repeat, like when she gave the same line a decade later about Demi Lovato and Ariana Grande, or when, after they broke up, she sued ex-fiancé James Packer for $50 million for wasting her time. It's delightful to read about, and maybe delightful for Mariah to enact, too, but this entertaining audacity can swerve sometimes into real loneliness.

After all, the Aries energy doesn't only materialize in moments when it's useful and welcomed. Aries isn't Aries only on stage or in the studio, when the world is open to being dazzled and brought to its feet. Aries isn't pulled to battle only when there are real battles that must be fought.

Aries is Aries in quiet moments, too.

Aretha Franklin is an Aries onstage at the Apollo, but she's an Aries, too, when reporters keep asking her unwanted questions and she just wants to get some rest.

Celine Dion is an Aries when she's demanding to sing in a turtleneck dress at the Oscars, but she's an Aries, too, when she's privately mourning the death of her husband.

Mariah Carey is an Aries every time she rockets up into her whistle register, and she was an Aries, too, in her emotionally abusive marriage with Tommy Mottola, keeping her bag with her at all times, as she told Aliya King in 2005, in case she needed to escape.

An Aries isn't an Aries only at the top. Sometimes an Aries is still striving. Sometimes an Aries is lonely and afraid. Sometimes an Aries is just a person who wants more than the world will readily give.

AND SOMETIMES, THE SO-CALLED ARIES prickliness doesn't come from anything inside the person at all. Sometimes it's an idea imposed from the outside, the view from a world that can't entirely understand or respect this energy.

Celine Dion's mighty exuberance elicits discomfort as

quickly as it elicits praise. In his book about Celine Dion, *Let's Talk About Love: A Journey to the End of Taste*, Carl Wilson catalogs a whole litany of insults: one-line zingers from critics, dubious "awards" from television shows and magazines ("most annoying song ever," "most annoying singer"), and even a dig from an episode of *Buffy the Vampire Slayer*. Some of the scorn is certainly born from a genuine distaste for Dion's music, but at the same time it's impossible not to wonder how much of it is gendered.

Aries is one of six astrological signs that is traditionally considered to be masculine. In many ways, Aries is the most masculine-coded sign of all twelve, ruled by Mars, god of war. In contemporary astrology, the "masculine" signs are sometimes instead called the signs with a positive charge: a direct, active, outward-facing energy. The "feminine" (negatively charged) signs carry an energy turned inward, an energy that's observant and receptive and magnetic.

Most astrologers will be quick to assure you that the astrological masculine and feminine have little relation to masculinity and femininity in our social world, and even less relation to any individual's gender. Even so, there can be a real discomfort in the world when a woman embodies these "masculine" traits: when she's too direct, too active a force in her own life. This means that often the best and most vital Aries qualities can be misunderstood: seen not as a valuable source of power but an embarrassing or irritating display of excess.

I think about the job I worked in the prepared-foods

kitchen of a small, fancy grocery store when I was twenty-three. The prep cooks were all young women, and we spent each day busy roasting chickens and assembling grain salads but also clowning and gossiping, enjoying each other's company and listening to music.

I remember specifically the days we played Aretha Franklin and Mariah Carey and Whitney Houston. (I don't remember listening to Celine Dion there, although it's completely likely that at some point somebody would've queued up "My Heart Will Go On," and we all would have taken a quick break from trimming the ends off green beans to swoon and sway and sing along.) These Aries musicians provided the soundtrack to a particularly joyful, assured era of my life—one where I thought happiness and love and everything good in the world could someday be mine.

Eventually our kitchen manager left and was replaced by a man who, unlike the rest of us, came from the restaurant industry proper—the macho restaurant industry, screaming-head-chef restaurant industry, aggressive-posturing-around-knife-skills restaurant industry. Doubtful of our competence in the kitchen, he wanted to give us all skills tests. Doubtful of our awareness of the world, he wanted to educate us about Occupy Wall Street and mass incarceration. He planned to write a book of cautionary parables about past girlfriends who had once been politically upstanding citizens but then, according to him, lost their way, becoming selfish airheads who dyed their hair. When he told these stories, it was hard not to feel that these weren't stories of people who had lost their morals or their political compass at all; rather, they sounded like stories of people whose ambition and drive and self-worth had blossomed, growing bright and unruly and entirely more than this man had ever bargained for.

Unsurprisingly, after some months, he confessed to us that he hated the music we played in the kitchen. He simply was not a fan of the whole "vocal Olympics" thing. He preferred music with . . . "a brain."

It's wild: these artists have spent years mastering their voices and techniques. They can create sounds inaccessible and unimaginable to most people. With nothing but the power in their own bodies, nothing but the air in their own lungs, they can fill a room with sound; they can bring a feeling to life in somebody else's heart; they can remake the world. There's something specifically Aries about the sheer act of filling your lungs and belting it out. And to be near an Aries can feel like a gift, the same way a song can feel like a gift. There's a powerful feeling that accompanies just listening to an artist like this, just being invited inside their bright vision.

But to the man in the kitchen, there was no pleasure here. He could recognize Mariah Carey's five-octave range as an Olympian feat, but it incurred no respect. I think of how the children at my school joked about Celine Dion's theatrical vocals with closeness and intimacy and something approaching love: we recognized the melodrama in the soaring key change, but still we moved our own bodies to mirror the emotions in her voice. This man grew up and could only see a headache, showy and distasteful.

Rejection and dismissal of women's art is by no means limited to Aries, of course; it's a classic variety of misogyny, and, to be fair, this man hated Beyoncé, a Virgo, just as much. But there's something illustrative here of the Aries struggle to be seen clearly in a world that does not quite know what to do with certain kinds of genius.

Sometimes the Aries gifts of power and courage and confidence are celebrated, but sometimes they're met with fear or anger or wild, irrational claims that they're simply unpleasant or too much. An Aries *can* be too much, of course. An Aries can be selfish, can be thoughtless. Sometimes, though, what looks like selfishness or excess is just a soaring, astounding mastery that we aren't yet ready to see truly.

THE MAN IN THE KITCHEN wanted to unionize our grocery store but only spoke to the men behind the butcher counter. He told me this once when our lunch break coincided and we both sat on the bench outside the store, eating sandwiches from the deli counter. "Everyone's just too terrified," he explained sorrowfully. He did not ask me whether I might be interested.

Angry, I asked others, and learned that he also had not asked the workers at the cash registers, or the workers behind the deli counter, or any of the women working back in the prep kitchen. At the time, I told myself this was a symptom of pure and straightforward misogyny: he saw us all as naïve children at best and insidious class traitors at worst.

Lately, though, I've started to consider the possibility that the reason he didn't ask us wasn't because he thought we wouldn't be bold enough for action, but because he feared that we *would* be. Is it possible that, in the same way he turned away from the courage and joy and mastery in the songs we played in the kitchen, he also turned away from our headstrong and unruly Aries energy of courage and creation in real life? I can't really know, of course, and it hardly matters now. But I wonder if things might have gone differently if he had known how to value courage when it didn't look like a masculine warrior but a laughing worker at a deli counter or a woman who dyes her hair.

Even the purest, most powerful, most glowing Aries energy can't single-handedly transform all the world's injustices into something good and bright and sweet. But when we're ready for it, Aries energy can offer us the courage to rise to meet our own ambitions. It can bring us to our feet and make us brave, too.

TAURUS

The Wrestler

*T*HE STORY OF FERDINAND, WRITTEN BY MUNRO LEAF AND ILLUSTRATED BY ROBERT LAWSON, WAS ORIGINALLY PUBLISHED IN 1936, AND IT'S THE MOST TAURUS STORY I'VE READ IN MY LIFE. It goes like this: Ferdinand, a young bull growing up on a farm in Spain, loves nothing more than relaxing in his meadow and smelling flowers in the shade of his favorite cork tree. The other young bulls love to romp and spar and play—they dream of being selected for the bullfights—but not Ferdinand. His mother worries about him initially—he's so unlike the other kids!—but understands that he's just different, and the thing that makes him happiest isn't the thrill of butting heads with the other bulls but the sweetness and luxury of life in the pasture.

It seems tragic, a setup doomed from the start: Ferdinand was born and bred not for softness, not to enjoy his time on earth, but to get strong and then fight and then die. When all the young bulls get big enough, men from the city travel to the farm to choose the strongest one among them for the bull-fights. Ferdinand has no interest in showing off his strength for them, but the pain of a chance bee sting makes him wild, running and stomping and huffing and puffing, suddenly strong and fearsome. The men see this and choose him for the fight.

When the day comes they parade him grandly into the arena, where he immediately sits down on the ground. His only interest is in smelling the flowers all the finely dressed ladies wear in their hair. (In Disney's animated adaptation, Ferdinand is also delighted by a daisy tattooed on the matador's chest.) But no matter what they do to try to make him fight—and it's implied, though not shown directly, that the standard methods for impelling a bull to fight include sticking him with pins and prodding him with long spears— Ferdinand simply refuses. The matador is so disappointed that he cries. Ferdinand is taken back to his meadow again, where he sits and smells his flowers under his beloved cork tree. The final line of the book: "He is very happy."

Ferdinand was the best-selling book of 1938, overtaking even *Gone With the Wind.* In February 1938, *Life* magazine reported that it wasn't only a kids' book anymore, and "three out of four grown-ups buy the book largely for their own pleasure and amusement." And, like any number of contemporary children's media objects consumed by adults—*Star Wars*, *Steven Universe,* My Little Pony—*Ferdinand* set off a storm of controversy. According to a 1938 *New Yorker* roundup of the hot takes, Ferdinand was accused of being a "rugged individualist," a "ruthless Fascist who wanted his own way and got it," and a "satire on sit-down strikes." Adults worried that Ferdinand was a bad example for children—a model of laziness, of antisocial behavior, of a terrifying softening of American masculinity. In their 1938 song "Ferdinand the Bull," the duo Slim and Slam sang "Ferdi is a sissy, yes, yes." In 1940, the Freudian journal *American Imago* published an article calling the Ferdinand story "a clear cut castration threat."

Ferdinand's author, Munro Leaf, always insisted that he had no particular political axe to grind; he maintained that he only wanted to write an enjoyable story for children and seemed frustrated by the volume of interpretive attention his book received. In 1939, the *Los Angeles Times* reported that Leaf was less worried about the charges of political propaganda than he was about attacks on his masculinity. As Bruce Handy wrote in the *New Yorker*, Leaf was concerned readers would assume his soft-hearted protagonist was a reflection of himself. "So he likes to have it known," the *LA Times* reported, "that he is a lacrosse player and won a boxing championship at Harvard . . ."

Even as late as 1951—more than a decade after Ferdinand's entry onto the best-seller list—Ernest Hemingway published a weird rebuttal in the form of a story called "The Faithful Bull"; "his name was not Ferdinand and he cared nothing for flowers." Hemingway's bull loves to fight—anyone, anytime, anywhere, even under the cork trees. He falls in love with the youngest, slimmest, most gorgeous cow on the farm and, to the farmer's frustration, refuses to breed with any of the other, less beautiful cows. At the end of the story, the anti-Ferdinand gets sent to the bullfights, where he dies a noble death at the hands of an admiring matador. This story offers a pointed vision of what a good bull should be, but it offers us no insights at all into the astrological bull, Taurus. For that, we have to look to the stubborn, disobedient Ferdinand instead.

There's a strong Taurean energy in Ferdinand's refusal to bow to anyone else's will—not the other bulls', not the matador's, not the audience's up in the stands. Ferdinand's contemporary critics read deeply into the political implications of this refusal: Was he refusing masculinity, refusing violence, refusing the existing social order? But as far as any discussion of Taurus is concerned, it hardly makes a difference. For stubborn Taurus, the refusal itself is the point. And while this *can* be about a principled refusal to be conscripted into morally objectionable activities, it can also be about a simple refusal to be bothered, a refusal to do what one does not want to do, a refusal to be forced—not by social pressure, not by internalized guilt, not by a matador threatening and pleading and waving his cape—into compliance.

Importantly, Taurus's connection to its symbol, the bull, is about much more than the bull's powerful horns and physical strength. While Taurus *is* a sign of earthly physicality, it would be a mistake to conflate—as Hemingway does—the bull's physicality with a rough, combative brutality. The bull also has those surprisingly soft eyes, long-lashed, deep melty brown, languid and intelligent. Ferdinand, more than any of his companions in the field, and more than Hemingway's one-dimensional fighter, embodies the strength and the stubbornness and the sensual delight in the world that Taurus is all about.

Taurus understands that life should be about more than toil, more than conflict, more than endless striving. Taurus is a sign willing to remind us of our very human right to enjoy ourselves here on earth. Ferdinand, as a representative of Taurus energy, *loves* his beautiful life and finds a deep satisfaction in basking in the sunny meadow, smelling every flower. If this is laziness, it's a sweet and deliberate kind, born not from weakness or apathy but from an active, immersive pleasure in the world of the senses.

Ferdinand's Taurean value system—preferring to enjoy his life rather than participate in a fight that would inevitably kill him—drove the cultural commentators of the time into a weird spiral of analytic anxiety. It isn't hard to imagine why. If you've fully bought into a particular way of living—if you've accepted, for instance, that masculinity means violence and domination, that suffering is worthy, that self-denial is a social good—it can be disturbing to be confronted with a different way to live, maddening to see someone who refuses to bargain away their own happiness, and still lives.

Taurus offers us an inversion of what Aries has to give. It grows out of Aries's aggressive exuberance and also tempers it, pushes back against it. If Aries is the sign of headstrong forward motion, Taurus is the sign of headstrong stubbornness. If Aries is the sign of sheer will to *act*, to move forward, Taurus is the sign of sheer will not to be moved. And if Aries can illuminate what becomes possible when a person unexpectedly embodies a bold, spiky, assertive power, then Taurus

can show us what it looks like for someone to refuse harsh-
ness and severity, and surprise us with powerful, tender sensuality instead.

WITHIN THE VAST AND SCATTERED landscape of internet visuals, there exists a GIF of the wrestler Chuck Taylor
(Chuckie T) standing in the corner of the ring, densely muscled and sweaty and yet so seemingly relaxed that it takes a
moment to even notice his opponent is there, too, slumped
against the ropes. Simultaneously, and smiling all the while,
Chuck pushes his opponent's head down, grabs him under
the armpits as though to haul him back into the center of the
ring, and says to the camera, languid and grinning, as if to
explain himself: "I'm a Taurus."

Participation in a combat sport seems, at first glance, totally opposed to Ferdinand's preference for bucolic nonvio-
lence, yet everything about this two-second GIF—the brawn
tempered with good-natured sweetness; the luxurious enjoyment of what one's own body can do—somehow still seems
to match. Of *course* this brawny musclehead with the seduc-
tive smile is a Taurus. Of *course* it would be a wrestler who
could show us, with intimacy and good humor, how to honor
the power and pleasure and possibility that our physical bodies hold.

After watching the Taylor GIF loop half a dozen times,
each time marveling at the sheer Taurus energy it managed

to convey, I curiously googled the names of the first few wrestlers I could think of: The Rock, then Andre the Giant, then John Cena. And all three have their sun in Taurus. (Incidentally, John Cena provided the voice of Ferdinand the bull in the 2017 animated adaptation.) As an afterthought, I checked Hulk Hogan, too. Turns out he's a Leo, although according to multiple (unverified) birth chart reports online, his midheaven—a placement that speaks to career goals and reputation in society—is in Taurus.

The thrill I felt at this connection had nothing to do with imagined causality; there is, obviously, no relationship between having a sun in Taurus and a career as a wrestler. Plenty of divas (Cher) and poets (Adrienne Rich) and philosophers (Karl Marx) have a sun in Taurus, too, and plenty of wrestlers have no planets in Taurus at all. Rather, it made me wonder if wrestling might be a space in which Taurean characteristics can excel.

Seen in different arenas, through different lenses, Taurean characteristics can be cast as undesirable: Taurus can be seen by some as stubborn, plodding, materialistic, or worse. As Ferdinand's critics showed, Taurus's desire for pleasure can be absolutely infuriating to those who associate goodness with self-sacrifice. But wrestling, like the Ferdinand story, offers a stage on which a Taurus can be praised for embodying Taurean energy. Here, Taurus's lush physicality can offer us a vision of a world in which our bodies aren't shameful or bad, and our own *enjoyment* of our bodies and what they can do isn't shameful or trite, either. Wrestling offers a stage on which Taurus can shine, on which Taurus can be positively heroic.

TAURUS IS AN EARTH SIGN, the first one of the astrological year. Considering a sign's corresponding element (fire, earth, air, water) is useful, because whether or not you're aware of this, you likely already know, more or less, what each one is all about. English is rife with metaphoric, idiomatic speech involving the four elements, and these typically line up very neatly with the elements' astrological meanings.

Earth signs, therefore, can be understood to be "earthy" in a way you probably already intuitively understand: grounded, practical, reliable. Earth signs are "down-to-earth"; they're "rooted." On a bad day, or surrounded by people who don't understand them, they can be perceived as "sticks in the mud." If the blazing fire signs, like Aries, experience the world most vividly through action, earth signs experience the world most truly and intensely through all that is material, all that can be touched. Generally speaking, earth signs tend to be attuned to the practical details in life; they don't lose their heads in the clouds or get washed away on a sea of emotions but instead focus on the real-life work that needs to be done. This often manifests as the reliability of habit: Taurus will take the trash out on the right day, or remember to water the plants in the window on a regular schedule, or show up to yoga every morning, day in and day out. Taurus isn't a sign that's likely to get so wrapped up in a task that they forget to eat, or work in short frenzied bursts followed by long, fallow periods. Taurus will do what needs to be done and do it habitually, reliably, well.

Earth signs also tend to have an innate feeling of rootedness in the physical body. This can look like an elevated attention paid to the things that they touch and wear and eat and sit in. It can mean a keen focus on the five senses and thus a desire to be surrounded only by things that feel good, look good, or smell good.

It can also look like a heightened attentiveness to one's own body. In the case of these wrestlers, it's easy to notice: they're tall and muscular, just stunningly huge. There's a myth that makes the rounds every so often that even as a young child Andre the Giant was so large that he couldn't fit on his school bus. It turns out not to be true, but it's a story that keeps coming back because it *feels* true that Andre's physicality was so exceptional that it demanded exceptional recognition from the world.

Caity Weaver's 2017 *GQ* profile of Dwayne "The Rock" Johnson, a Taurus, also gives special recognition to his physical form. He invites her to his private gym, where she marvels at the equipment nearly too heavy for her to pick up, lets him cheerfully convince her to lift weights with her neck (!) along with him, and looks at his workout handbook, a neatly handwritten document of the varying routines he can use to maintain his body or change his shape. There's no coyness here, no shying away from the fact that Johnson wasn't born into this bulk but works hard to create and maintain it. There's no apparent shame here at all over spending what seems like half his life in the gym. Why *wouldn't* he value his body? Why *wouldn't* he devote time to caring for it and treating it well?

The point isn't strength, specifically—physical largeness is as much a reflection of chance and genetics as it is a reflection of hours spent in the gym—but rather the careful and loving attention paid to one's own body. Some dreamier people can give the impression that their physical form is a burden or a surprising afterthought, but for Taurus it's the opposite. Watching a Taurus, you get the impression that the body isn't an afterthought at all but a central part of experiencing life. Even when Taurus is frustrated by their body, even when Taurus fully and miserably hates their body, as we all sometimes do, they remain grounded in it. They know that the body, and all the things it can do, all the sensations it can experience, is central to what it means to be human.

WITH THIS GROUNDEDNESS, TAURUS POSSESSES a power that lends itself well to resisting and defending and less naturally to attacking or initiating. It's one of the primary traits of Fezzik, Andre the Giant's character, an enormous and sensitive wrestler, in *The Princess Bride*. Employed in a small criminal outfit led by a shrill super-genius, Fezzik's job is largely to hold down the fort, metaphorically and sometimes literally, for the rest of the group. He's responsible for ongoing physical work, for heavy brute-force tasks, for using his strength to defend his friends. He scales a steep cliff with the rest of the group clinging, deadweight, to his limbs; he knocks out attacking villains with a single punch; he throws open an iron portcullis; through his sheer size he terrifies an entire company of the king's men into taking flight. He, like the real-life Andre—who was rumored to have flipped a car over, with four men inside it, after the men harassed him— isn't aggressive just for the sake of it but isn't afraid to fight back, either.

When his boss asks him to fight Westley, the story's hero, Fezzik offers Westley more than one chance to decline to fight at all; ever the Taurus, Fezzik finds no particular thrill in aggression or competition, and isn't motivated by a desire to prove himself better than other people. He knows his own strength and will use it if he must, but would greatly prefer not to hurt anybody. But as much as Taurus would prefer, ideally, not to get involved, this is a sign that won't shy away from conflict when it comes. When Westley rushes forward, throwing the entire weight of his body against Andre, it's as if he's rushing a stone wall, a fully immovable object. A Taurus comes into their own when resisting and defending their own boundaries, their own stubborn equilibrium. If attacked, Taurus can be steadfast. Taurus can refuse to be moved.

There's a similar moment in a 1982 WWE match where, Andre the Giant and Hulk Hogan team up to fight Bobby Heenan, Nick Bockwinkel, Ken Patera, and Bobby Duncum.

It looks like chaos in the ring, with so much whirling activity that it's difficult to count all the moving bodies, all the sweaty backs and blond heads. When the dust settles momentarily, Andre is visible in the corner of the ring, leaning back, nonchalant.

"All this time Andre the Giant looks like he's just relaxing," narrates the announcer, "but what he's doing is squashing one Mr. Bobby Heenan behind him into the turnbuckle." Heenan's hands reach out from behind Andre to swat ineffectually at his chest. Andre is unmoved. "Where *is* Bobby?" asks the second announcer. "He's hidden back there somewhere!" says the first.

Stillness can be deceptive. If you're not paying close attention, it can seem like inactivity, even laziness, when actually, all along, it's been power.

SOMETIMES THIS STILLNESS, THIS STUBBORNNESS, this steady earth-sign groundedness, can be misunderstood; we can look so hard for practicality that it becomes all we can see. We can mistake it for a *lack* of energy, not a *quiet* energy. Although it can be useful to be guided by metaphors and idioms related to the four elements, eventually it becomes limiting, too, as do all containers we try to place ourselves in. For earth signs in particular, it's easy to imagine "earth" to mean something like dirt, something boring, something dusty and dry. In reality, though, "earth" can be absolutely luxurious.

In her essay collection *Braiding Sweetgrass: Indigenous Wis-*

dom, Scientific Knowledge, and the Teachings of Plants, Robin Wall Kimmerer describes the revelation her university students experience when she brings them to the woods and shows them what wild forest soil actually looks like: not bland or dusty at all but rather rich and silky and dense, "so sweet and clean you could eat it by the spoonful." Her students *think* they know what soil is, but Kimmerer compares the vast difference between tilled garden soil and wild forest soil to the difference between ground beef and "the whole blooming pasture of cows and bees and clover." At the risk of sounding, somehow, simultaneously ghoulish and hippieish, Taurus isn't the pound of hamburger, either. Taurus is the living cow in the fragrant, blooming pasture. Taurus's deep connection to the physical world is practical, of course, but it's also—even more than the other two earth signs, Virgo and Capricorn—imbued with a rich sense of pleasure and of all the ways it's possible to enjoy life on earth.

This connection to the pleasures of the physical world comes from Taurus's ruling planet of Venus—beautiful, milky-white Venus, planet of beauty and love. It's also, somewhat surprisingly, the planet of money. This can seem confusing at first, as though it's inappropriate to mention love and money in the same breath. But in the case of Taurus, it makes sense. Venus isn't the planet of finance or capital; rather, this is the planet of money as it operates on a smaller, human scale. It's about the things you can buy with it, the ways you can, ideally, use money to experience life's pleasures.

For Taurus, this Venusian desire for pleasure and enjoyment can verge on the hedonistic, as in Andre the Giant's famed penchant for putting away hundreds of beers or entire cases of wine in single sittings. It can even verge on the silly, as in wrestling underwear with a bull emblazoned on the butt, like those The Rock wore when he fought John Cena at Wrestle-Mania XXVIII. Unlike Taurus's earth sign cousin Capricorn, Taurus's enjoyment of physical luxuries doesn't require things to be expensive or high-quality or "fine" or even impressive to other people at all. The signature denim shorts John Cena wore to that same match—medium-length, medium-wash, desperately uncool—hold their own funny luxury, the indulgence of untrendy comfort for nobody else's sake but one's own.

Beyond the costumes, wrestling creates space for another kind of physical spectacle. It isn't an arena for showcasing competition and sportsmanship. Rather, wrestling is all about the animal thrill of The Rock leaping off a ladder to crush an opponent, or John Cena picking up another large man and hurling him on the floor, or Andre the Giant defeating a dozen men in a tug-of-war. It isn't exactly about combat—the violence isn't exactly "real"—but it's not strictly performance or a kind of bulked-up dance: real injuries do happen sometimes. Wrestling is about narrative, but it's also about the pure physical fact of bodies crashing into contact with one another, and about the enjoyment we can derive from it.

IN 1938, *THE STORY OF FERDINAND* inspired a small-scale moral panic that the children of America would read the book and become soft, embarrassing weaklings. It was to these critics seemingly unthinkable and unbearable that a character might reject war in favor of sweetness, that someone might happily and unregretfully choose a life of pleasure over a life of violence.

In 2017, *The Story of Ferdinand* was adapted into a feature-length animated movie with John Cena, wrestler and Taurus, as the voice of Ferdinand. The movie includes a fleshed-out backstory, an extended bull-in-a-china-shop gag, and a cast of wacky supporting animals, but follows the same broad arc. In both versions Ferdinand is recruited into the bull-fight; in both versions he refuses. But by 2017, "following your heart" and "being true to yourself" are normal themes for children's media; Ferdinand's journey of self-discovery feels sweet and hardly subversive at all. And the culture has grown, naturally, in the eighty-plus years since the original picture book was published. We now have a robust language available to make sense of what precisely Ferdinand is resisting: "socially conscious adults in the audience," wrote the A.V. Club, for instance, "will pick up on Ferdinand's pointed jabs at toxic masculinity . . ." But the point isn't only about resisting the demands of toxic masculinity; it's about resisting all those who would tell us not to value our own bodies, our own pleasure.

At first glance it might look like wrestlers and old Ferdinand the bull exist on two opposite sides of a spectrum, but I think they're much closer than that. Wrestling, as it exists today, only *looks* like it's about the fight. Really, it's about the spectacle, the performance, the earthy delight in our physical forms. The link is Taurus-ness; the link is the space they create for power and strength without real violence, power and strength that can be sensual and grounded and *fun*. If the Aries divas model how a person can be loud and ambitious, these Taurus wrestlers show us how a person can be brawny and soft at the same time. These Taurus wrestlers show what it can look like for someone to choose what to do with tremendous stubborn power: they choose to fight, but they can also stand still. They choose to work, but they also choose to enjoy the miracle of existing in their own body.

And they can show us, too, how to value these things. Societies celebrate certain kinds of intelligence and denigrate other kinds, and don't even recognize some kinds at all. Meanings and associations accumulate so densely, they tangle before our very eyes, and suddenly we're imagining that feeling the sheer sweetness of being alive isn't a gift, isn't a skill, isn't worth anything much at all. Taurus can remind us that it is, and that there's a beautiful earthy magic in refusing to believe otherwise.

GEMINI

The Trickster

IN ASTROLOGY'S CONTEMPORARY ONLINE BOOM, GEMINI TENDS TO BE CAST AS ONE OF THE ZODIAC'S MAJOR VILLAINS: THE WILDEST OF THE SIGNS, THE LEAST RELIABLE, THE BRINGER OF MESS AND CONFUSION. In this meme-ified version of the world, Gemini may be charming, thrilling, absolutely delightful, but *beware*: you can't invite Gemini warmth and charm into your life without inviting its corresponding chaos, too. Donald Trump is a Gemini. So was his closest Canadian counterpart, the scandal-ridden former Toronto mayor Rob Ford, and so is his English counterpart Boris Johnson, who was once described in the *Guardian* as a "duplicitous scoundrel" and a "jester, toff, self-absorbed sociopath and serial liar." According to the stereotype, this is a person with no real emotional commitments to speak of, except for a commitment to stir things up and cause trouble; a person with a compass that doesn't stay pointing north but swings back and forth every time the wind blows; a person who can be convinced to say or do anything as long as it's interesting. Even Lizzo (a Taurus), queen of confidence and generous love, has publicly talked shit about the sign, as reported by Allison P. Davis in *New York* magazine: "This is for every woman-ah, who has ever-ah, been victimized by a Gemini . . . Should I slander Gemini? You know what? Yes. Give us a reason to like you, Gemini."

I want to get all this out of the way at the beginning, in order to acknowledge that you might be coming into this chapter with an assumption that all Gemini has to offer are bad exes and chaotic conservatives. Worse still, if you have strong placements in Gemini, you might believe that all astrology can see in *you* is this same kind of duplicitous villain. It's not true, of course. All the signs are equally good and equally bad; all of them are equally necessary pieces of a whole. There's no "worst" sign, just signs that suffer from particularly bad PR. In answer to Lizzo's provocation, there are plenty of reasons to like Gemini and to love, to respect, to cultivate the Gemini energy in ourselves.

As for myself, I came late to any awareness that Gemini was supposed to play this villainous role. My earliest and most abiding Gemini association was the name of a roller coaster in the amusement park not far from my grandparents' house in Cleveland. What made the Gemini special, and what gave it its name, was its side-by-side double tracks. Two trains, one red and one blue, traveled along the route at the same time, racing. As a tiny kid, before I knew anything about astrology, I loved Gemini, the roller coaster and the constellation. I thought it sounded like the name of a sorcerer, like a magic incantation. It sparkled in my ears; its syllables sounding like jewels, like crystals, the two dotted *i*'s like a pair of twinkling stars.

Generally speaking, a roller coaster isn't the worst way to conceptualize Gemini: not just the unpredictable metaphorical emotional roller coaster—although there might be some of that—but the real thing. A roller coaster offers a cool breeze on your skin, an excitement so pure and fun that people are willing to line up for it and wait. It offers the collective thrill of riding to the top of the crest and seeing the entire park laid out down below. It offers the shared comic delight of seeing everyone's laughing, screaming faces photographed at the moment of the big drop. It's about brightness and enchantment and speed, about a shared social experience.

The idea that Gemini's energy is bad and deceitful is a matter of interpretation; it's not an essential astrological law. The essential astrological elements that make up Gemini, in fact, hardly point to any kind of villainy at all. To return to the basics, Gemini is an air sign—the first of the astrological year, followed by Libra and Aquarius. Air signs are the signs of thought, the signs that experience life most vividly in the realm of reason, language, and communication. Air energy doesn't necessarily translate to scholarliness; a bright, electric air sign mind is as likely to tend to the imaginative as to the analytic, as likely to bend toward the dreamy as the intellectual. It's less about the style or shape that thoughts take than it is about the sheer fact that thought is how you process the world, that your electric mind is what makes you feel most vital, most alive, most yourself.

A general, metaphorical "airiness"—and the lightness and clarity that implies—can be a useful way to understand air sign energy. Air signs are able to move, quickly and easily, between different ideas. They're able to avoid getting stuck in the weeds, trapped by the details, hampered by a limited imagination.

Air signs are sometimes described as "shallow"—not because of a lack of seriousness but because they're more comfortable moving across a wide breadth of thoughts and fields of knowledge than plumbing the depths of a single question. While air-related idioms like "airhead," "space cadet," or "head in the clouds" suggest absentmindedness, the astrological air element is not about having a head empty of thoughts but rather, if anything, a head *too full* of thoughts—a mind moving so actively, so quickly, it's hard to see it land in one place for long.

Because Gemini is ruled by Mercury, the planet of communication and connection, its buzzing air sign energy takes on a particularly social element: communicative, charming, highly verbal. Gemini can be extremely likable, skilled at connecting, collaborating, and simply having fun with other people. Additionally, because Gemini is a mutable sign—these are the signs that come at the end of a season and are flexible, adaptable, and comfortable with change—it is particularly adept at being a social shape-shifter, adapting to seamlessly fit into nearly any situation. Gemini can move between friend groups and social scenes, as natural and charming at the fine dining restaurant as at the dive bar, as easily gregarious in first class as they are on the Megabus. Gemini can quickly and brilliantly determine what a person wants to hear and then say exactly that; they perceive what someone wants them to *be* and then become—at least for the moment—exactly that person.

This ability to shape-shift can sound like a tool of trickery and deceit, but it isn't only that. In the Greek myth of the twin brothers Castor and Pollux—the story most closely connected to the constellation of Gemini—it's quite the opposite. In the most common version of this story, Castor and Pollux share a mother but have different fathers, and while Castor is mortal, Pollux is divine. After Castor dies, Pollux begs Zeus to let him stay together with his brother; he offers to share his immortality, or even relinquish it, if he can just stay with Castor. Zeus grants them immortality of a kind: they can't keep their current shapes, but they can stay together in the night sky, the two bright stars in the constellation Gemini. By persuading Zeus to change his shape and his destiny, Pollux pulled off a classic act of Gemini trickery—motivated not by malice or deception but a deep loyalty to his other half.

In both real life and in the stories we tell, this inseparable twin loyalty can seem unsettling to the point of appearing practically supernatural. Twins report communicating telepathically; twins report feeling each other's physical pain; twins report communicating, as children, in private invented languages. Twins, to the outsider, can seem to meld and separate again at will—dressing alike, talking alike, mirroring one another's movements. Twins can swap places just because—just to see if anyone notices. If Schrödinger's famous cat remained simultaneously alive *and* dead until the experimenter opened the box to find out, Schrödinger's twin can be both people, simultaneously, for as long as you don't know which person you're looking at.

This magic isn't necessarily frightening. Children's and young adult literature is packed with books featuring bright-eyed, adventurous twins—from the Bobbsey Twins and the Sweet Valley High twins to tricksters Fred and George Weasley in *Harry Potter*. In these stories, being a twin was presented, overall, not as some kind of strange and cursed mystery but an incredible gift. To have a children's-book twin was to have a constant companion; a person always there to chat with, argue with, develop harebrained ideas with; a friend who'd be down for anything with you. This is one shape that an ideal Gemini life might take: to never have to be lonely, because from the very start and to the very end, there's a friend right there to talk to.

The prolific perfecters of this variety of wholesome twin story—at least, to my microgeneration of Old Millennials—are real-life twins and Geminis Mary-Kate and Ashley Olsen. They started acting as babies on the sitcom *Full House*, on which they played a single character between the two of them, the tiny and precocious Michelle. They found new stardom effortless and natural and established their own production company by the time they were eight. Between 1993 and 2004, their company would produce thirteen movies for them to star in. And whereas *Full House* collapsed the pair into a single character, eliding their twin-ness, these new movies would center it. Each movie had its own plot, its own characters (in *How the West Was Fun*, twins Jessica and Suzy try to save a dude ranch from a greedy developer; in *Switching Goals*, twins

Sam and Emma trade places on their rival soccer teams), but the story at the movie's beating heart was often the same. These were two twins with contrasting personalities—smart versus sporty, social versus shy, ambitious versus boy-crazy— learning to reconcile their sameness and their differences, each character learning to grow into herself while loving her sister, too.

And if generous, companionable sister love was these movies' beating heart, then hijinks were their lifeblood. In *Billboard Dad*, for instance, the twins engage in constant scheming to find a girlfriend for their single dad. In *Our Lips Are Sealed*, they accidentally steal a diamond from a crew of bumbling jewel thieves and must work as a duo, dressed in coordinated outfits, first to elude the pursuing thieves, then catch them. All the trickery hums with Gemini energy: these characters don't try to overpower or outmaneuver, for the most part; rather, they chat, they charm, they persuade. And, just like in the story of Castor and Pollux, there's an underlying, motivating loyalty to each other.

This motivating loyalty appears, too, in *It Takes Two*—one of only two of their movies released into theaters, rather than directly to video, and the only one in which the twins don't actually play twins. *It Takes Two* is part updated *Prince and the Pauper* and part bootleg *Parent Trap*, with Mary-Kate and Ashley as a pair of identical strangers who meet by chance at a summer camp. In this iteration of their contrasting personalities, Ashley is a prim but good-hearted rich girl, whom we first meet performing Chopin in a sumptuously decorated concert hall. Mary-Kate, in contrast, plays a wise-cracking, gum-chewing tomboy whom we first meet in a stickball game outside the Brooklyn children's home where she lives. Ashley lives with her single dad; Mary-Kate dreams of being adopted by her kindhearted caseworker.

They discover each other at the summer camp for disadvantaged youth that Ashley's rich father owns and soon decide to temporarily trade places: Mary-Kate wants a chance to experience what it's like to live in a home with a parent who loves her, and Ashley wants to escape the stuffiness of her life and have some fun for once. More importantly, they hatch a scheme to sabotage the engagement of Ashley's dad to a selfish socialite and instead set him up with the caseworker.

Their mischief includes a disastrous piano recital and a food fight in the camp cafeteria, and at the end they crash into the church at the last minute to stop Ashley's dad from getting married. Armed with their cuteness and charm, the twins persuade the dad and the social worker to fall in love; we're meant to conclude that, after the end of the movie, the grown-ups will get married to each other, they'll adopt the orphaned Mary-Kate, and everyone will have what they wanted for so long: love, an end to loneliness, warmth, togetherness, and a life full of fun.

Here, the Gemini trickery wasn't only well-intentioned; it was in the universe of the movie, the only tactic that could have set things right again. When inertia sets in too powerfully—

the father trapped in his wrong relationship, the social worker trapped in her loneliness, everyone trapped in a life with no luster, no sweetness, no thrill—it takes a jolt of chaos to bring the world to life again, to set everybody free. And, more than just about anyone else, it's Gemini, with all its curiosity and boldness and aliveness to the world's opportunities, who can provide that necessary push.

IF *IT TAKES TWO* IS a close cousin of *The Parent Trap,* the actual *Parent Trap* is a Gemini story, too, even without twin Geminis to star in it. Rather, in *The Parent Trap,* we get one actor split into two selves: Susan and Sharon in the Hayley Mills–led original, and Hallie and Annie in the 1998 remake starring Lindsay Lohan—who is, according to multiple celebrity birth chart websites and an unverified nugget of "Trivia" from IMDb, a Gemini rising. (Her sun is the softer, more emotive, more contained and private Cancer.)

Playing these twinned roles seems like a specific kind of Gemini dream—indeed, like a Gemini miracle. Your true self suddenly becomes doubled, expanded. Here, Lindsay Lohan plays twins separated at birth who (also!) meet by chance at summer camp. Both twins are initially disturbed to find their own face on another person, alternately ignoring and competing with the other. But Gemini is not, ultimately, a sign that thrives on pointless competition or jockeying for status; Gemini is energized less by success or attention than connection. And no matter how hard the twins try to hate one another, they can't help but connect.

After fully acknowledging that they're twins, the two girls make a plan to swap places at the end of the summer, teaching each other the details of their lives, training each other in their mannerisms: nail-biting, a posh English accent, a slouchy American posture. One gets a haircut; one pierces her ears. They're offering each other access to lost versions of themselves: refined Annie gets to experience herself as a rangy Californian in flannels and jeans, and tough-girl Hallie gets to experience feminine softness with a mother who loves her.

Gemini's antics have a purpose beyond simply shaking the world free again. Gemini's behaviors aren't typically about hogging the spotlight or stealing the show. They are, just as often, motivated by generosity, by a desire to let other people shine alongside them, to allow other people to share in their glow, to feel equally brilliant and exciting, equally full of charm and life. At its best, Gemini's brightness shines onto you in a way that illuminates *your* brightest self as much as theirs.

Although, to be fair, of course, these antics can without a doubt be put toward more devious purposes, too. A Gemini can use their social acuity to wreak social havoc. In the service of reuniting their parents, the *Parent Trap* twins run circles around their father's young and selfish fiancée. Social and observant, they know exactly how to frustrate her, how to manipulate her greed and vanity, and how, ultimately, to defeat her. In their final trick, they bring her on a camping trip with them and their father. On the hike, they covertly torment her, leaving a lizard on her water bottle, fooling her into using sugar water as insect repellant, convincing her that beating sticks together will fend off the threat of mountain lions. They do all this while appearing, to their father, as though they've been nothing but cheerful and kind.

This offers a glimpse of how Gemini's duality can slide into what might be less generously called two-facedness. And, indeed, other contemporary twin narratives seem more interested in this element of two-faced deception than in the loyal siblinghood on display in the Olsens' stories. Secret and/or evil twins—twins, in other words, as bringers of mystery and our dark other halves—remain mainstays, to the point of cliché, in soap operas and science fiction. On *All My Children*, David Canary starred as a pair of twins for thirty years—one gentle and artistic, the other greedy and devious. *General Hospital* has an entire page on its fan wiki listing pairs of fictional twins who have appeared on the program to create drama and excitement, to punch up a plotline's chaos factor. The characters on various *Star Trek* shows are constantly being confronted by their mirrored selves from parallel dimensions, finding their humanist ethics refracted into ruthlessness, their confidence amplified into foolhardiness, their selves made simultaneously familiar and unrecognizable.

In these stories, the twinned self poses a potential threat: Once you become aware of the twin's existence, can you ever again *really* be sure whether you're dealing with your friend or her devious and power-hungry twin? With your partner, or her unpredictable doppelgänger? So much of what pop astrology has to say about Gemini implies a similar threat: Can you really trust what your friend is saying, or are they simply telling you what you want to hear? Can you really trust a person who charms you so easily, or will they turn around and, the moment you're not looking, charm somebody else just as easily? It can feel destabilizing to not ever know for sure, to love somebody so good yet so changeable.

Gemini's shape-shifting power also creates an uncomfortable space where our own selves become destabilized, too. Do we actually know who we are, or do we contain unknown multitudes as well? Are we really ourselves, or might we turn around to find secret parts of us coming up to the surface? Gemini reminds us that we're not stuck in place forever. Gemini reminds us that we can reverse direction, that we can change our minds after all. Gemini reminds us that we can be surprising to even ourselves. By offering us the possibility, always, to choose and change, to always be both, what Gemini does is offer us a bigger world.

ULTIMATELY, SO MANY OF THE fears surrounding Gemini are fears of some kind of *too-muchness*. People are often made uncomfortable by others who seem to want to know

too much, do too much, *be* too much. People are often un-
nerved by change and those who thrive in it. Gemini's adapt-
ability can read, to these people, as a sign of artificiality or
untrustworthiness. Gemini's duality can even seem threatening, based on false binary thinking that a person can only
have a "good" side if they have an evil side, too, and can only
have a "real" self if all other selves are treacherous fakes.

And while a Gemini might not particularly care what others think, that doesn't mean that they don't notice. After
all, Gemini is ruled by Mercury, the planet of communication, and communication never flows only in one direction.
Gemini—whose skill in communication lies not only in expression but also in observation—definitely notices when it's
being undervalued and misunderstood.

In spite of all the trickery, Gemini does want, at the end
of the day, to be seen and understood. And in spite of all the
airy lightness, Gemini has a real center, a real self, a heart that
beats like anyone else's. The fear, for Gemini, is that they'll
be forced to reduce their true self to fit somebody else's idea
of what a person can be—to choose just one piece of their
full humanity. It's not exactly an unfounded fear: there are
so many forces in the world that would prefer that all of us
choose just one thing, just one way to be, just one easily,
narrowly defined self. But, for Gemini, the broad, complicated, contradictory self *is* the true and essential self. "Do
I contradict myself? / Very well then I contradict myself, /

(I am large, I contain multitudes)," wrote Walt Whitman, a Gemini.

THERE'S OFTEN A SCENE IN the Olsen movies where the twins—having already traded places, having charmed their way across a new city, having tricked their way into their goals—find themselves afraid that they'll no longer be recognized for who they actually are anymore. In *Passport to Paris* (1999), for example, twins Melanie and Allyson visit their stuffy grandpa in France and end up meeting two French boys. Each twin develops an intense crush on one of the boys, and the four of them arrange to meet up at a dance. Right before the boys arrive, the twins express their shared apprehension: Will their new crushes be able to tell them apart? Will they be able to see them clearly? It's important. At the end of the day, they both want and deeply need to be known and recognized, to be seen clearly. And in this movie they are. The boys pass the test: as they arrive at the club, each heads directly toward the correct love interest as though pulled to her by an unerring magnetic force.

This particular happy ending is hardly the point. Rather, it's about Gemini's ability to show us that, in spite of all the anxiety around it, embracing our own contradictions doesn't have to lead to sorrow. There are plenty of reasons to like Gemini: for their quick and observant mind, for their willingness to shift and change as the world changes, for their ability to be a little too much. A Gemini can show the rest of us, too, that we can change our shape and change our mind; we can be entirely too much, and we'll still be whole, we'll still be ourselves. We can refuse to be predictable, refuse to stop moving, and still remain worthy of love.

CANCER

The Poet

IF YOU EVER FIND YOURSELF SEARCHING ON THE INTERNET FOR POEMS ABOUT LOVE—MAYBE FOR A WEDDING TOAST OR AN ANNIVERSARY MESSAGE; MAYBE JUST TO MAKE YOURSELF *FEEL*—YOU'RE PRACTICALLY GUARANTEED TO FIND HIT AFTER HIT OF PASSAGES FROM POEMS BY PABLO NERUDA, A CANCER. An image search, in particular, will bring you to the really good stuff: the lovestruck and lovelorn posting Neruda text over stock photos of roses; the wedding planning websites with Neruda quotes over stock photos of wedding cakes; Neruda's work rendered in typewriter or handwriting fonts and his name in elegant, flowing script. He seems wildly adored by young people pining for love, by wedding vow writers, by people searching for a mirror wide enough to reflect their own vast love back to them.

"Tonight I can write the saddest lines," begins a poem that shows up with particular frequency. "I love you," goes another, "as one loves certain obscure things; / secretly, between the shadow and the soul." Or, more titillating: "I want to do with you what spring does with the cherry trees." Severed from their literary context, transposed into a novelty font and placed on clichéd photographic backgrounds, images like these can seem corny and stale. Looking at too many of them in a row can give a person the same sick and empty feeling of having eaten too many sweets. But even the maudlin can gesture, if imperfectly, to something real. The initial silliness of the images themselves can serve as an ungainly outward expression of a poetic feeling that runs true and deep.

A poem can take many different shapes—story or song, riddle or manifesto—and perform many different kinds of magic. One kind of magic is the creation of a doorway—a portal no bigger than a thumbnail-size image on a search screen—directly to our deep and vivid feelings. A poem can be a tool for making our feelings knowable and bearable.

This relation to poetry—as a release valve for loneliness, a vessel strong enough to hold the desire that spills out of our bodies—tends to be ascribed most often to teenagers. Our emotions are more dazzling and unruly when we're young; we haven't yet built up the tools needed to neatly process them. We haven't yet hardened our hearts, haven't been worn down by the long-term, repetitive grind of the world. At least, this is how the common wisdom would have it.

And it was true, to an extent, for me. Factually speaking, my external teenage life was basically unexciting, but my inner world felt mysterious and alive and nearly too bright to look at, too much to bear. Poetry offered me a window to a world equally alive, to the thrill of a deep and private feeling, to the space between the shadow and the soul. Poetry offered a doorway into the thing I wanted more than anything else: a life full of depth and expression and endless, fluid emotion.

Living for emotion, though, can lead a person into intolerable vulnerability. American high schools operate as though expressly designed to make it dangerous to publicly show weakness, softness, any emotion at all. It feels safer for everyone to tighten their defenses, keep their soft places hidden, and show real feeling only fleetingly, with a trusted friend, far away from the group. Or better still: show the feeling to nobody at all but let it out secretly in a poem instead.

Years after high school, I found out my rising sign was Cancer, and the description of the sign validated all the sadness, all the brooding sensitivity, all the years of lovesick whining. It offered me one explanation for why, no matter how hard-edged I had tried to be, I kept returning to softness, to poetry, to carefully inscribing *"Tonight I can write the saddest lines"* in my lonely teenage diary. Cancer is the sign that teaches us to respect our inner emo teen, and it's also the sign that shows us what happens when we nurture that emo teen into a loving, feeling adult.

IN OUR MODERN SKIES, CANCER—the dimmest constellation of the zodiac—is represented by a crab. In Greek myth, Cancer is associated specifically with the crab that Hera sent to sabotage Heracles when he fought the Hydra. To thank the crab for its service, Hera placed it among the stars. But Cancer hasn't always been seen as a crab. Over time, it's also been a tortoise, a scarab, a water beetle, a crayfish, a lobster, and in one seventeenth-century depiction, according to Richard Hinckley Allen's 1899 text *Star Names: Their Lore and Meaning*, "a small shrimp-like object." All of these incarnations, with the exception of the scarab, have been water dwellers—which is fitting, as Cancer is the first water sign of the zodiac year.

Water signs experience the world most directly through feeling: rather than thought or physical sensation, it's emotion that offers water signs the clearest way of understanding the world. For these signs, feelings are as solid, as useful, as real, as any kind of imagined "rationality" in the material world.

Just as feelings morph and swell and change shape, so do they offer a way to access our secret selves, ourselves as they exist beyond and beneath the rules of the everyday, the rules that govern our physical bodies, the rules of how we think we *should* be. Water signs experience the world in a way that is fluid and changing: dreamy, intuitive, and highly sensitive to what goes unspoken. They can relate to the world with an emotional fluidity, with the rolling wisdom of the tides.

As with the other elemental energies (fire, earth, and air), our language already easily expresses the water sign's qualities. In writing about his youth in *Memoirs*, for instance, Pablo Neruda makes offhand but illuminating nods to water more than once. His shyness—simultaneously intensely oppressive and intensely dreamy—is "rain-haunted." Pining after girls, he imagines their intoxicating mystery—and his desire for them—as a deep well that he'd gladly drown in.

Yet "watery," in this context, shouldn't be taken to mean weakness—as though water signs are simply watered-down versions of some other, stronger brew. Water sign energy is powerful and deep. It's as magic, as magnetic, as salty as the sea. Here, the water isn't a neutral, diluting agent. The water *is* the power; the water itself is the point.

BEYOND LIVING IN WATER, ALL of Cancer's historic incarnations—even the tortoise, even the shrimp—have some kind of exoskeleton, some kind of hard outer shell. This shell is one of the most abiding Cancerian images: the defensive mechanism, the built-in system for protecting oneself against the outside world. The shell is often understood to mean shyness and a lack of confidence; it's conceptualized as a limiting force, a barrier to a rich and healthy social life, something one must learn to "come out of." More generously, the shell can be thought of simply as a tendency toward privacy, an appropriate guardedness, a useful protective adaptation.

In *Memoirs*, Pablo Neruda uses the metaphor of the shell as well, describing himself as "a mollusk leaving its shell" when he moved out of his first city room. "I said goodbye to that shell," he writes, "and went out to explore the sea—that is, the world." He also writes about the shell of his own shyness as an intensely limiting force. He declined to talk to girls, although he was desperate to, out of fear that he'd stutter or blush, instead feigning a total lack of interest to cover up the true intensity of his desire. Or at home he'd listen intently to conversations between his father and his father's guests, yet ignore those same guests if he ran into them outside the safe shell of the house. The shyness was an "inherent suffering," the feeling of the shell so intense and so real, it was "as if we had two epidermises and the one underneath rebelled and shrank back from life."

Neruda's shy and shelled-off temperament is far from unique among poets. But where Neruda's shyness eventually receded, the purportedly intensely private nature of Polish poet Wisława Szymborska, also a Cancer, extended well into adulthood and the height of her career. She avoided literary conferences and events; Clare Cavanagh, one of Szymborska's English translators, told the *New York Times* that Szymborska was "kind of paralyzed" when she found out she'd won the Nobel Prize: "Her friends called it the 'Nobel tragedy' . . . It was a few years before she wrote another poem." A day after winning the Nobel, Szymborska declared that she planned to relocate to somewhere remote enough in Poland that nobody could find her.

It would be a misunderstanding, though, to think of the Cancerian "shell" only in relation to the outside world. It's also about protecting a rich, complex, endlessly fascinating inner life. For Cancer, one's own interiority is a wild and secret treasure. Neruda called his shyness a "damaging thing" but also part of the "foundation, in the long run, for the perpetuity of self." A meaningful life need not rely on things outside the self—on attention or social connection or tangible successes. Cancer's inner life doesn't demand to be performed loudly or publicly, doesn't need to be validated by others before it can be experienced as real; it can be felt and experienced deeply to the fullest degree, even if nobody's looking at all.

CANCER'S RULING PLANET IS, NATURALLY, the most poetic of all the planets: the moon. (Remember that for the purposes of astrology, if not astronomy, the moon is a planet.) In the birth chart, the moon—along with the sun and rising signs—is one of the three most important placements and influences one's private, inward-facing self. As the fastest-moving of all the planets, spending only a couple days at a time in each sign, it's the planet of our shifting, changing moods and emotions. It's also the planet that determines what a person needs to feel loved, protected, cared for, and safe. If the sun's blazing, assertive heat can sometimes feel harsh, the moon's light is gentle, cool, silver, and more magnetic. The moon is close enough for us to see its surface but far enough to remain mysterious; bright enough to cast a glow through the night but not so bright as to dispel the darkness. Moonlight can be haunting, intimate, romantic; it can induce a soft, poetic state in a person.

The moon is also classically associated with the feminine. More specifically, it's associated with a cosmic, archetypal motherhood. The moon—and therefore Cancer, the sign it rules over—is thought to be the bearer of gentleness, of care, of a love that's safe and good and luminous in the night.

Under the feminine, mothering power of the moon, Cancer is thought to be made of soft, gentle curves rather than sharp edges. Cancer's boundaries are more porous than hard. It's not a sign of discipline or strictness or cruelty, not a sign of worldliness, but rather one of nurture and selflessness, its sights oriented toward home and family.

The association of Cancer with motherhood is about archetypes, not real, in-the-flesh people. Archetypes are ancient and enduring, larger than any one of us; they exist in a space that goes deeper than logic or argument can reach. But in real life, this conflation of Cancer and the Mother can often be more complicating than it is illuminating. We're not great, collectively, at respecting the border between the archetypal and the human; it's almost impossible not to let mother archetypes bleed into our thoughts about, and expectations of, real-life mothers, who are expected to be boundlessly selfless and infinitely loving—responsible, as Gemma Hartley complains in *Fed Up*, for keeping everyone else in the family happy, comfortable, and cared for. The archetypal mother's priority is to give care to others; from there, it's easy to expect that real mothers, too, will prioritize the family, never her own needs and desires, or her own ambition, or her own pain.

Likewise, it's almost impossible to stop our culturally produced ideas—informed less by the heavens than by the movies, by our politics, by the history of the last century—from infiltrating our archetypes. Our culture and our archetypes change and reinforce one another, shaping the stories we're able to tell and the ways we're able to see. As much as we *know*, in our rational minds, that ideas of archetypal motherhood are vastly too big and too heavy for any real person to bear, much of our culture persists in using the archetype as a yardstick to measure actual people.

Without keeping some careful distance from it, the archetype can become a prison for actual mothers, and Cancers, too, and it can limit the ways we're able to understand how soft, nurturing, protective, love can act in the world. Because all astrological thought is a reflection of the human world it came from, plenty of astrological resources offer outdated, regressive, strange ideas about motherhood, gender, and love— and thus, by extension, about people. It's a vision of astrology, and by extension the universe, in which everyone is cis and no one is gay, in which mothers are loving and fathers are tough, in which every awful, limiting structure we've built here on earth gets refracted all the way out to the edges of the galaxy. When archetypes of masculinity and femininity become too literal, and in turn when this rigid way of thinking gets attributed not to human culture but to the enduring, natural will of the universe, it can be hard to find any space left for actual human people.

It isn't that calling Cancer the sign of the Mother is *untrue*— only that the association isn't a simple one. It limits our understanding as much as it adds to it. There are ways, of course, to push back. Maggie Nelson offers one model in *The Argonauts* as she lovingly and expansively describes her teachers, mentors, role models, and friends as the "many-gendered mothers of [her] heart." Still, I crave the space to imagine Cancer energy in a way that's neither explicitly linked nor more unconsciously, nebulously tied to our real-life mothers or real-life children.

How can we understand Cancerian love—tender, intimate, nurturing, wise—in a way that doesn't rely on natalism or reproduction or the nuclear family at all, even in archetypal form? How can we understand Cancerian love that's true to family as we actually experience it—not limited to bonds of blood, or to the people you could claim on your taxes, but inclusive and open to change? How can we imagine a Cancerian love in which an orientation toward family, in which a deep and abiding love for family, isn't a mark of a conservative outlook, or a sign of a refusal to engage with the broader world, but a *way* to engage with the broader world, with a soft and tender strength?

IMAGINING CANCER NOT AS THE sign of the Mother but the sign of the Poet breaks open a different interpretive space, one not explicitly gendered, one not required right from the start to contend with the fraught social space occupied by the nuclear family. Thinking of Cancer as the poet helps us access another Cancerian intimacy. This can offer a different kind of air to breathe, a different way to envision what Cancer is capable of. It can offer a different way to envision what it might look like for someone to be intently focused on their rich and imaginative inner life, and on the vast and secret universe of the human heart.

Neruda offers one example of the emotive Cancerian poet, with the massive popularity of his intimate love poems. Wisława Szymborska does, too, in her lifelong movement away from the collective-minded socialist realist work of her youth and toward poetry she described as "strictly not political," focused on the shades and nuances of life and feeling. Fellow Nobel-winning poet and fellow Cancer Czeslaw Milosz told the *New York Times* that Szymborska's early "Stalinist phase" was not particularly good, but that her work kept getting better as it tightened its focus to the personal, noting with approval the reserved and refined nature of her poetry and personality: "It is just a whisper."

When Szymborska won the Nobel Prize in 1996, the committee praised her "ironic precision" that allowed "the historical and biological context to come to light in fragments of human reality." This is not, in other words, a poetry purporting to be *without* historical context, but it weaves that context quietly into the fabric of interior life, with nuance and richness and depth. Her poems invite readers into this quiet space with her, into this water-sign depth, into this state of poetic feeling. For ultimately, as she said in her Nobel speech, to be a poet is to turn away from the distractions of the world and into the inner life: "The moment always came when poets had to close the doors behind them, strip off their mantles, fripperies, and other poetic paraphernalia, and confront—silently, patiently awaiting their own selves—the still-white sheet of paper." Behind these closed doors, the poetic Cancer is able to value the deep over the merely noisy, the true over the merely convenient.

But the poet, of course, isn't a clean slate for creating meaning, either. Like all human activity, poetry has its own fraught social history. It comes with its own set of built-in conceptions and misconceptions, its own set of troublesome, impossible ideals. It brings with it its own world of figures who were canonized and uplifted despite themselves, and those who were silenced, ignored, forgotten in spite of their worth.

Quiet, intimate, apolitical poetry is far from the only kind of poetry that is published, and it's far from the only kind of poetry that is great. It was, however, for many years the type of poetry that had most been elevated and canonized in the modern English-speaking world. It's the poetry that's been anthologized and taught in schools, the poetry that's been held up as the best of the genre: private, focused on a particularly intuitive, particularly emotive person's experience of life. To be any good, goes this line of thinking, poetry must not be political nor serve a specifically moral or didactic purpose. Rather, the mystery of the inner life is poetry's domain.

And although Cancer exemplifies the traits of a traditionally, private, internal poet, it can also show us a way into a different kind of poetry entirely, one that looks inward toward
the self while looking out to the world, too. One that speaks
to the ways that personal feeling and worldly matters are inextricably bound up together. A Cancerian disposition—with
its ability to feel deeply, its deep love for family—doesn't have
to lead to a walled-off reclusion but can lead a poet *into* their
community, their world, their shared struggle. All the Cancer love and emotion doesn't stop existing once it enters the
broader world, so what can it do in public? What can it do in
the busy, noisy world of other people?

Pablo Neruda's political trajectory—the inverse of
Szymborska's—offers one example. While Szymborska, disil-
lusioned by eastern European communism, moved away from
the overtly political, Neruda's work—and life—became more
political over time, not less. His work developed in a direction that brought him closer to the political world—and the
world of other people. He wrote poems praising communist
leaders like Stalin and Fidel Castro. He wrote poems against
the colonial violence enacted by multinational corporations
in Latin America, going so far as to call out by name Coca-
Cola, Ford Motors, and the United Fruit Company—and not
in a statement or essay but in the poem itself. When Neruda
won the Nobel Prize in 1971, the committee's announcement
acknowledged that it might be controversial to award a writer

willing to break the norms of poetry like this, calling Neruda a "contentious author who is not only debated but for many is also debatable."

Neruda himself, in spite of the beauty and lyricism and feeling of his love poems, plainly rejected the idea that poetry should *only* be about beauty or lyricism or feeling. As he wrote in 1966, he believed poetry could provide not only lofty feeling but a more earthly, nurturing care: "a poetry of bread, where everyone may eat."

June Jordan, who once noted with some amused frustration that Neruda's contemporaries consistently described him as a "quote unquote poet *despite* the political commitment of his art," was a Cancer, too. And Jordan, like Neruda, steadfastly insisted on a poetry that nurtures even as it looks fiercely outward toward the world. She resisted the idea that emotion is something watery and soft, tender and private, something to be held inside oneself, guarded like a precious and terrible secret. For Jordan, poetry was always inextricably bound up in the world around her. Her poetry—like her essays, like her YA novel, like her collaborative work with R. Buckminster Fuller, like the workshops she ran for young people in Brooklyn—was not only a way to express a feeling but a way of caring for the people in her world: her family.

In a 1978 essay, Jordan wrote what could be Cancer's guiding principle: "As I think about anyone or any thing— whether history or my father or political organizations or a poem or a film—as I seek to evaluate the potentiality, the life-supportive commitment/possibilities of anyone or any thing, the decisive question is, always, *where is the love?*" Cancer doesn't have to be reclusive or retiring, or soft and nurturing, or easily undone by emotion; nonetheless, Cancer is keenly aware of where the love is and where it's not, keenly alive to love's potential.

Jordan's work suggests a way to stop fighting the idea that Cancer is oriented solely toward home and family. She doesn't renounce or resist the home; she doesn't try to disown or distance herself from tenderness and love. Instead, she expands the definitions. "My life seems to be an increasing revelation of the intimate face of universal struggle," she wrote in the foreword to *Civil Wars*. "You begin with your family and the kids on the block, and next you open your eyes to what you call your people and that leads you into land reform into Black English into Angola leads you back to your own bed where you lie by yourself, wondering if you deserve to be peaceful, or trusted or desired or left to the freedom of your own unfaltering heart." Home is never really as small as the four walls of a house, and family doesn't have to be as small as one's partner, or children, or blood relatives at all. We're all connected to each other; our families here on earth are huge, if we'll just let them be.

Cancer shows us how a life guided by feeling might look—a life where we grow up and out from our emo teen selves but don't then become hardened, or unfeeling, or selfish. Cancer can show us how feeling might continue to guide us, through our loneliness—as behind Szymborska's closed doors—and through our connection; through our soft vulnerability; through an ever-expanding world of people worth caring for, and back to our own hearts, our own inner worlds, to our vast and abiding secret selves.

LEO

The Director

IN THE SUMMER OF 1992, FILMMAKER SANDI TAN, A LEO, WAS EIGHTEEN, LIVING IN SINGAPORE, AND DREAMING OF A LIFE FREE FROM CULTURAL PRESSURES TOWARD CONFORMITY, A LIFE FULL OF EXPRESSION AND ART. She became obsessed with *The Catcher in the Rye*, sure that children hold the answers to the world's mysteries that the staid adults around them have forgotten. She wrote for an underground rock zine, then created a zine called *Exploding Cat* with her best friend, Jasmine Ng. She watched every movie she could find. "When I was eighteen," she would say many years later, in her 2018 documentary *Shirkers*, "I had so many ideas I hardly slept at all." And what she wanted, more than almost anything else, was to make her own movie.

Sandi, Jasmine, and their friend Sophie signed up for a film class and became friends with the teacher, a strange American expat named Georges Cardona. He was significantly older than they were but treated them, Sandi felt, like they were his peers, like their ideas mattered. After class, the three of them and Georges would hang out and talk; they'd drive around; they'd dream about movies, about art, about life. Their home of Singapore felt small, but the future felt welcoming and wide, full of possibility and creativity and light.

Sandi kept in touch with her friends when they all left Singapore to attend college in England and the US. She also kept in touch with Georges, and when she finally wrote her screenplay—for a serial killer/road movie—she sent it to him, her mentor and friend, to read. In the script, the sixteen-year-old protagonist, S, who is "kind of a Grim Reaper," as Jasmine describes her, travels around the tiny country of Singapore, selecting people she loves to kill and bring on a magic journey in the afterlife.

"You . . . fuckin' Genius," Georges responded to Sandi in a fax, and, along with Jasmine and Sophie, they decided to make the movie. It was a deeply ambitious project for three teenagers and one weird adult with no institutional backing. Especially because Sandi didn't just want to *make* the movie. She wanted it to be *good*, to put Singaporean cinema on the map. And she wanted to do all this in just one summer, before everyone returned to school again in the fall.

"It was less than two and a half months," Jasmine says in an on-camera interview.

"Preproduction," Sandi clarifies, off-screen.

"No!" Jasmine corrects her, sounding incredulous that Sandi would so fully misremember the project. "Preproduction and shoot. For a *feature*. While most of us were still working day jobs." Jasmine and Sophie had wanted to wait a year to make the movie, but Sandi—with Georges's support—just wanted to charge forward and *do* it. "You have always been a very determined and quite ambitious person," Jasmine tells Sandi. "You just wanted it done at any cost, and you were willing to just burn things just so that you could make your own film."

MOST BASIC ASTROLOGY RESOURCES WILL introduce the sign of Leo using words like "regal" and "dignified" and sometimes even "conceited." "Hardworking" and "active" and maybe sometimes "bossy." "Creative" and "stylish" and possibly "dramatic," too. Leo is all about expression and leadership; put these qualities together, and they add up to the figure of the movie director. And not just any movie director but the big-name Hollywood blockbuster director: Alfred Hitchcock was a Leo, and so was Stanley Kubrick. James Cameron is a Leo. Christopher Nolan, David O. Russell, M. Night Shyamalan, Richard Linklater—all Leos.

It offers a neat contrast with Cancer, the sign immediately preceding Leo in the zodiac. Where Cancer is the sign most aligned with poetry—sensitive, intimate, focused on feeling and the inner life—Leo's nature, as made visible by the filmmaker, is more social, more commanding, more immediately expressive. And where Cancer is ruled by the dreamy moon, Leo's ruling planet is the sun itself—the focal point around which everything orbits, the bright ball of energy that warms the whole world. It feels almost unfair that any one of the signs should have as its ruler the entire *sun*, but if anyone best exemplifies all the sun's warmth, its power, its absolute life-giving sweetness, it's Leo. This is the object whose gravity guides the orbit of all other objects in our solar system; the object that guides our days, our years, our seasons, here on earth. This is the object whose light feeds our gardens and forests, and whose light we see by.

LIKE ARIES BEFORE IT, AND like Sagittarius to come, Leo is a fire sign, experiencing the world most readily and most naturally through *action*. Fire signs tend to share traits of spontaneity, boldness, creativity. And Leo in particular, among the fire signs, is likely to hold a special kind of hot, bright creativity, a special kind of electric energy. Leo is likely to be expressive—not subtly or quietly but in a way that demands and holds the attention of a room.

Other fire signs, too, can often be boldly expressive—think about Aretha Franklin's voice; think about Celine Dion's insistence on that long turtlenecked Oscars gown—but for Aries, this is more likely to stem from an inner drive too strong to be held in. Aries might like the attention, but that isn't, ultimately, the *point*. For Leo, on the other hand, integration with the social world is a key part of this creative energy. There's joy in connecting, in seeing and being seen, in engaging with the reactions of other people. For a Leo, expressing the self is important but incomplete on its own. For them, it's hard to see the point of personal expression if there's nobody there to see it. What's the good in telling a story, or dressing in beautiful bright colors, or making a whole movie, if it doesn't connect with anyone, if nobody is there to be affected by the warmth of your bright love?

This might make Leo sound like a sign that operates from some kind of deficit, hungry for external approval and unable to find satisfaction within. But that's not necessarily true, and it misses the point. For Leo, this need for human

connection—to be seen and known and loved by others—
isn't a hindrance, but one of the great joys in life, maybe
even one of the primary purposes of living. And why *shouldn't*
Leo find meaning in connection? Why shouldn't Leo do all it
can to experience the world's love, and to share that golden
light with the rest of us?

THIS SOCIAL ELEMENT OF LEO'S life-giving, sun-powered
energy also gives Leo its aura of leadership and its willingness
to call the shots. This is more than just independence; it's an
ability to lead others. Not everyone is comfortable or willing
to exist in the center of the action, or to be accountable for a
group, or to be the person others look to for guidance. Leo,
though, often is. It's about more than being looked *at*—it's
about being looked *to*; it's more than receiving attention—it's
using and directing all that attention, too.

And these are all useful qualities for a director to have.
While poetry, for example, can happen in solitude, behind a
closed door, making movies requires legions of other people.
Most types of movies require, at every level, the physical and
creative labor of other people. Even the punkest, most indie films—even a movie with the lowest-fi aesthetic and the
grimiest production values possible—still require someone
in front of the camera and someone behind it. And, to state
the obvious, the fancier a production gets, the more money
gets involved, the more eyes on the film, the more labor is

needed, getting into the critical jobs that people sometimes chuckle at, unbelieving, when they really pay attention to a movie's credits for the first time: Gaffer? Best boy? Foley artist? Managing and motivating all these people requires leadership; it requires a person to amplify their energies externally, express their creative vision publicly, and lead other people into making that vision become real.

James Cameron, for instance, had to ensure that the *Titanic* set was built exactly to specification to be historically accurate, and he had to direct Leonardo DiCaprio to play Jack Dawson with the right amount of sweetness, *and* he had to convince the Fox executives to let him take a submarine down to the actual wreck of the *Titanic* to shoot. Christopher Nolan could write the script to *Inception* on his own, but to bring the movie to life—to make characters move through bendy dreamscapes and fantastic cities; to make the city of Paris fold on top of itself—he had to work with whole teams of artists and experts and organizers to film car chases and foot chases and explosions and moments of quiet drama across six different countries.

Even in 1992, Sandi Tan needed the support and labor of other people to bring her vision to life—and not just her friends Jasmine and Sophie and Georges but other friends, neighbors, little cousins. She needed Sophie to finagle her way into getting free film to shoot on. She needed her musician friend to create a soundtrack. Incredibly, it worked, and they actually succeeded in shooting their film in just that one summer. The footage is utterly beautiful: shots full of life and movement, a color palette of faded tropical pastels—Sandi in a pink sailor shirt, plaster walls painted in blues and yellows and oranges, a man opening a briefcase lined in pink fabric, filled with brightly colored toothbrushes. A nurse and a shaggy dog dance together on a nighttime patio. Three tiny masked children dance in front of a painted iron gate. Sandi, as the main character, lies on her back in the lush green grass, gazing up into the sky.

BUT LEO LEADERSHIP RUNS ALONG a spectrum, ranging from the democratic to the dictatorial, the benevolent to the tyrannical. The line can be quite thin, between Leo in its best form—the inspiring leader who can persuade a roomful of businessmen to pay for a submarine voyage to the wreckage of the *Titanic*—and Leo in its shadow side—the autocrat who won't allow you to believe in anything *but* his personal vision.

And when it comes to movie directors, the general cultural narrative has long tended to elevate certain kinds of leadership, top-down and individualistic, with the idea that these Leo characteristics—the power of their leadership, the sunny warmth of their creative vision—can justify all manner of workplace tyranny. These are the stories about movie directors acting like the infallible kings of their sets, directors treating their crews like something less than human and their actors like raw material.

Alfred Hitchcock, for example, could be notoriously rotten to his actors. His harassment of Tippi Hedren on set is well documented; even off the set, he tried to control her career, keeping her under contract but refusing to cast her. David O. Russell is known for throwing tantrums on set and shouting at his actors; Amy Adams said he made her cry almost every day of filming *American Hustle*. Stanley Kubrick was famously demanding—according to Kubrick lore, he once had Tom Cruise film ninety-five takes of walking through a door for *Eyes Wide Shut*. While filming *The Shining,* he allegedly had Shelley Duvall and Jack Nicholson film the baseball bat scene—in which Nicholson, unstable and terrifying, menaces and berates the exhausted Duvall while she defends herself with a baseball bat—127 times. In a 1980 interview with Roger Ebert, Duvall, a Cancer, describes how hard she worked in the role, screaming and crying twelve hours a day, every day. And even after all that work, she says, Kubrick, the Leo, the sun, got all the attention. "Hardly anyone even criticized my performance in it, even to mention it, it seemed like," she said to Ebert. "The reviews were all about Kubrick, like I wasn't there . . ." Ebert gently suggested that it had nothing to do with herself or her performance, that maybe having such a big star in the director's chair made the critics "get mesmerized by his name and forget the actors."

This is Leo's power but also its shadow side: the power to command attention, but also the ability to devour all the attention in a room, leaving nothing left for anyone else. The power to get things done, but the ability, too, to leave your collaborators wondering whether, along the way, they were really even noticed, even listened to at all.

And the really strange thing is that for certain people, in certain contexts—for instance, among filmmaking's most powerful directors—Leo's shadow side isn't rejected but rather celebrated. Anecdotes about a director's famously difficult personality are recounted breathlessly in culture reporting, in profiles of actors who suffered their antics, in film studies classes. For some people, this shadow side becomes part of filmmaking's allure, part of Leo's mystique—something to strive for; not really a shadow side at all.

AFTER SANDI TAN AND HER friends shot their movie—after all the organizing, all the labor, all the vision, all the creative work and creative joy—Georges disappeared, and he took the footage with him. They had agreed that at the end of the summer, when the three girls returned to school, Georges would keep the film to edit it; instead, they never saw him again.

But they did, eventually, recover the footage: in 2011, nearly twenty years after the summer they shot the movie, Georges's widow contacted Sandi Tan to return the film reels—every single one of them—which she had found among Georges's things. Not only had he kept them, but he kept them safe and in good condition, perfectly preserved for nearly two decades and over thousands of miles, from Singapore to Louisiana.

Sandi visited Georges's widow in Louisiana to recover the film and talk to her. Georges must have known that his theft and disappearance would haunt Sandi, would change the shape of her ambition, her love of cinema, her whole creative life and career. So why did he do it?

His widow could hardly answer these questions, of course, but one thing she said was that he had a pattern of lying about everything—absolutely everything, even matters of clear, verifiable fact. Like, for example, his date of birth. He told people his birthday was two days after it really was. "He was really a Cancer," she said. "But by making it two days later, he got to be a different horoscope." Specifically, a Leo.

Sandi also met with another former protégé of Georges whose filmmaking career Georges also derailed. His theory was that, although Georges wanted very much to make his own movies, he could never quite complete the projects he dreamed of. And because he couldn't do it himself, his energies pooled and festered inside and he turned inward, turned rotten, and out of this jealousy he turned his energies toward blocking and destroying the projects of people who *did* possess the qualities that he imagined lacking in himself.

But it's hard not to wonder about the horoscope lie: it's seemingly such a tiny thing, and *Shirkers* presents it as evidence of a tendency to pointlessly lie about even the most inconsequential and easily verified facts. But it's hard not to wonder whether this particular lie indicated something deeper. Maybe Georges saw something specific in the sign of Leo that he wanted to emulate: Leo's creativity, or its outgoing warmth, or its sunny generosity. Or maybe he misunderstood. Maybe he only really wanted the shadow side, the power, the ability to rule over his projects like a king, first benevolent, then withholding.

GEORGES CARDONA MIGHT HAVE MISUNDERSTOOD Leo in this way. I once deeply misunderstood Leo's power, too—seeing only what was big and loud and unafraid—and this misunderstanding led to the great heartbreak of my life. Not with a partner or a lover but a friend who is a Leo, who loved me and then stopped.

It feels important to disclose that my vision of Leo might be shaped by pain and by love. This is true to some extent, of course, for all the signs. We can never understand them except through the lens of our own emotions and experiences, by paying attention from our own singular, subjective positions. What we see is messy, mixed-up, and personal, and this personal specificity can often be a strength. But when people with certain sun signs hurt us deeply—when heartbreak becomes involved—it's easy for our vision to become distorted, so that a sign's most powerful, or most frustrating, or most difficult traits are the only ones we can see.

In my case, it was the bright and powerful Leo traits that first drew me to my friend. We met in college, and I thought she was like the sun. Where I wore dark colors and wrote poems in secret, she dressed in neons and thrifted florals and danced harder than anyone else at the basement indie rock shows. Where I kept my opinions carefully, stealthily to myself, she spoke hers loudly, with confidence. At least, this is how I remember it now. I thought she was the coolest person I might ever be friends with. I thought her brilliance and her love could make me better, and they did.

When we graduated and couldn't find jobs—this was during a recession, and we had liberal arts degrees in the humanities—we moved to Brooklyn together, turning a one-bedroom into, roughly, a two-bedroom by stringing a bright sheet across the living room. We were both hired at the same company across the Hudson River and commuted together to New Jersey, where our glossy suburban coworkers thought we were strange and possibly dating each other. We weren't, but we spent all of our time together, going to parties and protests, dancing at shows, doing laundry together down the block, where our clothes—mine dark, hers bright—spun next to each other in the machines. And I felt doubly powerful with her, my Leo friend, because she let her sunlight shine on me. Leo thrives on receiving attention but is generous in giving it, too. Leo can offer a power, a warmth, a shared feeling of being bright and vibrant and alive in the world.

Although it felt different at the time, there was nothing

unique or surprising in the story of the breakdown: ordinary roommate problems (mismatched levels of tidiness—I was the messy one—and low-level irritation with a person you spend too much time with) and ordinary human differences grew into wild, unruly, unstoppable resentments. I felt constantly, relentlessly judged and grew evasive and distant; our friendship grew worse, less generous, less open. Although I still loved her, and still sometimes felt the old bright warmth, it seemed to arrive less and less frequently, and in its place rose up a stony coldness that left me feeling as though I might freeze to death from the lack of her Leo sunlight, the lack of her warm and generous love. This is, after all, how a person gets their heart broken: to be offered something wonderful and then lose the wonderful thing. To find something shining and radiant and life-giving, and then to have it broken.

My understanding of the situation at the time was that she had decided that the person I was—messy, annoying, weak—wasn't good enough. Not good enough for friendship and maybe not even for respect. And I believed this for a while. I became fearful that unless I shaped up, unless I became someone other and better than I was—less restless, less messy, more reliable—I could never expect to deserve a miraculous friendship like that again.

I left the city and spent years working my way out of a seemingly bottomless well of grief and insecurity and maudlin thoughts about my own unworthiness. It wasn't until much later still that I could wonder whether I'd gotten her all wrong, too—whether I had deeply, fundamentally misunderstood this particular Leo's nature. Because of Leo's sheer authority and *bigness*—its regal confidence, its imposing leadership—it can be harder to see Leo's deep vulnerability.

Even though Leo's authoritative nature and expressive dramatics can seem like a desire to control the room's attention, the deeper motivation is just as likely to be a desire to be appreciated and seen—a desire to be loved. Under the veneer of leadership and confidence and warmth, Leo can be one of the softest, most vulnerable of all the signs.

For so many years I thought the issue was that my friend needed to lead and control me, and withdrew her love when I proved too disorderly for that. I thought I was the one who was freezing to death from lack of kindness. But I wonder now if she was freezing, too. I wonder if the real issue was simply that she needed me to love her, and I was never clear enough that I did. Things might have been different if I hadn't been too lax about offering my own attention, too careless about expressing my love, until it was too late.

IT'S AN EASY ENOUGH MISTAKE to make about Leo, just like it's easy enough to find evidence of the autocratic temperament in directors: they certainly get enough attention for their difficulty. It's easy, always, to seek and find evidence for just one part of a sign's energy and to mistake that part for the whole. Maybe, when Georges Cardona was involved in the original *Shirkers* movie—trying to be a director and pretending to be a Leo—he just didn't want to see any other ways a director could be. Maybe, with so many highly praised and difficult role models, he *couldn't* see.

More and more, there's space to question our collective cultural myths about what leadership should look like. There are directors who can display as much of the Leo confidence and pride and vision as Stanley Kubrick ever did, while fully embodying Leo's warmth and love, too.

Greta Gerwig, for example—a Leo—has described in interviews what an absolute joy she finds it to be on set, working long, grueling days together with her team. "To be with my cinematographer, my first assistant director, and then all my actors, watching them bring these characters to life . . . I didn't see any reason not to create an atmosphere to reflect the joy I felt while at work," she said to BuzzFeed about filming *Lady Bird*. "I'm just crazy about them. I love watching them work." It's an entirely different mood than that of Kubrick, the genius moving his pawns around the board.

Gerwig's public image as a director still emphasizes her Leo characteristics, but they look different from those central to Hitchcock, Kubrick, and David O. Russell. In the same Buzz-Feed interview, she tells a story about being unable to find any suitably serious, boss-like, auteur-y photos of herself to use for publicity. "I'm always crying behind the camera, or laughing—I'm just in it. That was my experience of directing: just being totally emotionally tied to everyone on set."

This is what the best of Leo love looks like—committed, connected, giving—and it can feel like the brightest love in the world.

There's a moment in the middle of *Shirkers* where Jasmine calls Sandi on her bullshit. Sandi tells a story about her actions and motivations while they shot the original movie, and Jasmine cuts in to issue a correction. "You were obviously being an asshole. You've always been an asshole. Just as much as you have the capacity to be really wonderful, you have as much capacity of being an asshole." Maybe more than anything else, this is what Leo offers us: the capacity to risk being an asshole without being permanently defined by it—and the capacity, too, to be wonderful, generous, loving beyond measure. Because Sandi Tan, a director and a Leo, didn't have to include Jasmine's line in the final cut of the movie. But she did.

VIRGO

The Witness

CLOSE TO THE KNIVES: A MEMOIR OF DISINTE-GRATION BY DAVID WOJNAROWICZ, A VIRGO, OPENS WITH SEX (NOT WOJNAROWICZ HAVING IT, BUT THE IMAGINED SCENE OF HIS OWN CONCEP-TION, A "CALCULATED FUCK") AND VIOLENCE (WO-JNAROWICZ GETTING SHOT AT). He describes hunger and bleeding gums and hustling in bathrooms in Midtown Manhattan. He describes the seventy-year-old who used his disability checks to pay Wojnarowicz for sex once a month, and the "fetishist" who would make him dress up in an army sergeant's uniform and curse him out. He describes going to the Salvation Army soup kitchen and being served "mucus water." He offers stories about the world and its knotted cru-elties, its tiny mercies. His style, in the book's early essays, is rangy and impressionistic, the sentences stretching long, breathless, barely punctuated. He tells us about grimy New York and his travels in the big-skied American West, and about the skin-prickling pleasures and heart-thudding dangers of sex with beautiful square-jawed strangers. His gaze is sharp and critical. This is a writer who has seen the world in its smallest, harshest, loveliest detail, who can't forget what he's seen and who won't look away.

Close to the Knives was published in 1991, one year before Wojnarowicz's death. As the book progresses, Wojnarowicz's style becomes terser, more angry, more sad. He writes about losing his friend, mentor, and lover Peter Hujar to AIDS; he writes about the day-to-day work of caring for sick friends; he writes of the eventual numbness that came with losing friend after friend, acquaintance after acquaintance, love after love after love. From the beginning, Wojnarowicz was political in his ideas, but the later chapters become more urgently confrontational, more specific in focus not just on existential questions but on people, governments, policies. "What does one make of government policies if those policies let people die by saying those people die because they want to? What if those people are screaming for help as they die?" he wrote.

Wojnarowicz was a painter and a visual artist, too. His unfinished film *A Fire in My Belly*, which showed ants crawling on a crucifix, so enraged the founder of the American Family Association that he engaged in a national campaign in 1989 to protest the National Endowment for the Arts, which had provided funding to Wojnarowicz. By 2010 the film still packed a confrontational punch and was removed from a show at the National Portrait Gallery after a right-wing outcry.

He was also, by nature and by necessity, an activist. One of the most widely shared images of Wojnarowicz on the internet isn't one of his paintings or a still from one of his films but a photo taken of him by fellow activist Bill Dobbs at an ACT UP protest in 1988. Wojnarowicz, seen from behind, wears a black denim jacket with white text emblazoned over a pink triangle: IF I DIE OF AIDS—FORGET BURIAL—JUST DROP MY BODY ON THE STEPS OF THE F.D.A. In *Close to the Knives*, he imagines something similar: "if, each time a lover, friend or stranger died of this disease, their friends, lovers or neighbors would take the dead body and drive with it in a car a hundred miles an hour to washington d.c. and blast through the gates of the white house and come to a screeching halt before the entrance and dump their lifeless form on the front steps." These are the questions motivating so much of his work: How could he make other people see the violence he had seen? How could he communicate just how violent the government's lack of response to the AIDS epidemic really was? How could he bear witness?

STONE BUTCH BLUES, A NOVEL by Leslie Feinberg, also a Virgo, opens with violence, too: in a letter to an old lover, the narrator, Jess Goldberg, remembers long years of homophobic violence at the hands of "drunken gangs of sailors, Klan-type thugs, sociopaths"—but, most of all, the police, who regularly bust the gay bars where Jess finds community, harassing, beating, and sexually assaulting the bar's patrons.

The opening letter sets the tone of what the rest of the book will bring: an unflinching willingness to recount, in intimacy and detail, the full sweetness and the full brutality of Jess's working-class, lesbian, gender-nonconforming life. Jess knows she's "different" from a young age: her parents send her to a psych ward when they find her wearing her father's clothes. In high school, boys from her school rape her on the football field. Jess finds safety and community in the bars in

Buffalo, where other butches offer her friendship and a model for survival, and femmes offer tenderness, solidarity, and love.

Jess works manufacturing jobs and helps organize unions with workers—sometimes other butches but often men— who regard her with varying levels of understanding, fellow feeling, and trust. She falls in love with women who have varying levels of love to offer in return. She moves in and out of apartments, in and out of jobs, in and out of love, and always the violence—or the threat of it—remains threaded through the moments of sweetness and love.

Stone Butch Blues refuses to soften the violent physical realities of working-class queer life in mid-century America; it bears witness and demands that we look, too. And at the same time Leslie Feinberg has been careful about just *how* we're demanded to look. The twentieth anniversary edition of the book includes a small note at the front: "*Stone Butch Blues* is an anti-oppression/s novel. As a result, it contains scenes of rape and other violence. None of this violence is gratuitous or salacious." Leslie Feinberg also refused to release film rights to the book, stating that ze considered it once, before learning the producer was pitching it to investors as "a sexual fantasy: an invitation to watch butches being raped by police." The book, ze is very clear, isn't an object of anthropological scrutiny, or "an expression of individual 'high art.'" Rather, it's a "bridge of memory." It's an act of witness.

David Wojnarowicz and Leslie Feinberg might feel like odd selections in a more or less lighthearted book about astrology.

They represent such heaviness and grief. But one of Virgo's gifts, and one of the things it asks of the rest of us, is not to look away from sorrow or violence, not to pretend that the world is healthy when it's ailing. Maybe you've heard that Virgo is the sign of straitlaced, naïve perfectionism or of fussy, detail-oriented fastidiousness. It's true that Virgo is a sign alive to the importance of details. But this is a power that can be put toward more than just folding socks or alphabetizing the spice rack. Pay attention, and Virgo can start to look like the sign best situated, the sign with a cosmic gift or a cosmic duty, to bear witness.

VIRGO IS A SIGN THAT can be difficult to see clearly, in large part because of the meanings and images that cluster around the word "virgin." The Virgin, as in *The 40-Year-Old* . . . The Virgin, as in "who can't drive." The Virgin, as in Jeffrey Eugenides's lovely teenage suicides. The Virgin, as in "Is Britney Spears still one?" The Virgin, as in every boy in every teen sex comedy trying his hardest not to be one anymore.

The images and symbols associated with each sign matter. It's not random that Aries has the assertive horns of a ram, or Gemini the duality of a pair of twins, or Cancer the hard exoskeleton and tender insides of a crab. The signs aren't arbitrary lists of personality traits. They're cohesive assemblages, tightly linked networks of symbols and images and contradictions and balances. It's not possible or necessary to elide or ignore the word "virgin" and all its weird baggage—just to reconsider the lens we're viewing it through. The word isn't empty; it matters. But how can we understand it in a way that doesn't require us to keep breathing the air filled with all the same old cultural toxins?

Try to imagine you've never once watched a movie set in an American high school or been enrolled in an American middle school. Imagine that you've never once watched or heard about heterosexual porn. Imagine that when you were young, nobody ever once made you feel weird for having sex, or for not having sex, or for thinking about it. Imagine that there's no such thing as American evangelical Christianity, no such thing as promise rings, no such thing as abstinence-only education. Imagine there's no such thing as misogyny.

Cutting through the cultural sludge that clogs up our understanding of astrology is not a task unique to our understanding of Virgo, but Virgo does pose some unique challenges. Only a few signs are symbolized by a human figure—Gemini, the Twins; Aquarius, the Water Bearer; maybe, if you wanted to stretch it, Sagittarius, the Centaur—but Virgo is the only one of these, and really the only one of all the signs, whose symbol is gendered so intensely feminine.

And Virgo was gendered feminine before it was even called the Virgin. Ancient Babylonian astrology knew part of what we now know as the constellation Virgo as "the Furrow," representing Shala, goddess of grain, fertility, and the harvest. Early Greek astronomy associated the constellation with De-

meter and Roman astronomy with Ceres—both also god-
desses of agriculture, the harvest, and fertility. Virgo also
became associated with Persephone, who was kidnapped by
Hades but returned in the springtime with the grain (and who
is celebrated at the time of the harvest). These stories hold
close to one another with their overlapping themes of harvest, abundance, and the earth's fertility. It's unknown how
this figure of mature fertility came to be called the Virgin.
Some writers have claimed that Virgo came to be associated
with the Virgin Mary in medieval Europe; others suspect the
switch from mother to virgin to have been Greek or even Mes-
opotamian.

The point isn't when and why the Virgo figure evolved from
its ancient origins but that the shift is evidence of a complex,
layered, evolving history, evidence that our relationships with
knowledge, with religion, with sexuality and the feminine,
are changing and evolving all the time. If it's difficult to read
"the virgin" clearly through all our present anxieties about
our unruly human bodies in the social world, that isn't Virgo's
fault. It's on us to get our heads on right, even in a culture
that's obsessed with female sexual purity and the supposed
lack thereof.

As much as astrology interacts with the social and the
cultural—it's a way of understanding ourselves, and our selves
are deeply, irrevocably shaped by the places and times we live
in—the planets themselves are unmoved by our social rules.
As much as it seems obvious that "the Virgin" is symbolic,

not something to be taken literally, its meaning is slippery and the boundaries between the symbolic and the real are porous and leaky. There's an idea that Virgo tends toward the naïve—if not mentally, then physically. But some of the most affecting scenes in *Close to the Knives* describe Wojnarowicz as a boy engaged in survival sex work in New York. Some of these are brutal, some of them sad, some painfully tender, in the manner of a bruise.

Likewise, some of the most moving scenes in *Stone Butch Blues* describe Jess experiencing and learning through sex. Not wildly, not luridly, but not shamefacedly or uncomfortably or with a childish innocence, either. We read about the first time Jess has sex with a woman, all the thrill of it, all the awkwardness. We see the word "dildo" four times and "cock" three, and although it's an erotic scene, it's not at all lurid or sensationalistic or meant to titillate. It's just Feinberg telling the actual physical truth about a moment between these two characters. They're both young and they've both already suffered more harassment and violence and abuse at the hands of cops, family, and strangers than anyone should in an entire life. "By the time we're old enough to have sex," says the woman, Angie, "we're already too ashamed to be touched. Ain't that a crime?" But Leslie Feinberg, a Virgo, a wise and experienced adult, isn't ashamed to tell it truly.

Virgo is rooted in the body, but not in the sexual awkwardness of adolescence or the childlike naïveté of inexperience. It's emphatically, as Jessa Crispin writes in the Spolia Tarot,

not the sign of the "wispy virginal maiden, which is gross."
If there is some of the young maiden in Virgo, there's always
also the old maid, the nun, the crone, the spinster. There's the
wise witch, living in a hut in the forest or a rent-controlled
apartment, who pays attention to everything, who lets nothing escape her notice.

AND JUST AS VIRGO ISN'T the sign of the pure young
maiden, it isn't a springtime sign. Rather, it marks the end
of summer, the final sign before the autumnal equinox marks
the beginning of Libra. Virgo is associated with the harvest,
with the tangible results of the summer's long hot days. Based
on Virgo's strong associations with the harvest—and with the
physical world in general, including the body—it's an earth
sign, along with Taurus and Capricorn. These are the signs
marked by practicality and structure; they're also the signs
most closely attuned with our physical bodies and with the
physical world we live in. These are the signs most likely to be
described as grounded or dependable, the ones most likely to
keep projects organized and get solid results. The earth signs
aren't likely to be washed out to sea by the tides of their feelings, or swept away by the winds of their ideas, or burned up
by their fiery enthusiasms.

Virgo is associated with the harvest's bounty—all its abundance of color, of wisdom, of experience—because it's a sign
willing to do the work of earning it. And beyond just being

willing to do the work, Virgo thrives on being productive and useful. It's a sign that needs a solid, practical purpose on earth. For a Virgo, doing a job right means nailing every detail; often, this meticulousness is seen as Virgo's defining trait. Even at Virgo's most imaginative, most creative, most weird, Virgo is unlikely to let the heady thrill of having an idea get in the way of the details on the ground. To a Virgo, it's not chaos but order that makes the world come alive, not mess but clarity that allows new possibilities to make themselves known.

It's easy to find everyday physical evidence of Virgo energy: socks folded neatly in the drawer, an organized desk, a color-coded planner, an inbox zero. When I worked with a Virgo in a kitchen, she never added too much or too little salt to a dish, never left a pan of vegetables in the oven too long, never forgot to check the temperature of each roasted chicken and record it in our logbook. When I worked with a Virgo in a legal aid office, she noticed the errors on our documents and forms; she kept her workspace neat, every paper filed, and every tool returned to its proper place at the end of the day.

But this energy is about more than just everyday organizational strategies. Virgo's not only focused on orderliness, but on a deeper kind of goodness. Virgo's insistence on doing things right might initially look like simple rule following, but look more closely and you'll see that this isn't about deference to external authority. Virgo is unwilling to follow the world's rules when those rules are immoral, but Virgo will be steadfast and unswaying in following their own personal code of integrity. After describing an intense and life-giving sexual experience in a car on a dusty service road in Arizona, Wojnarowicz imagines what would have happened if the police had shown up just then: "I thoroughly believe that they have no right and that their laws don't reflect me." He continues a bit later: "Because I am born into a created system of corruption does not mean I have to turn the other way when the fake moral screens are unfurled. I am just as capable of creating my own moral contexts." He has no respect for the unjust laws of an unjust world, but will follow his *own* carefully considered rules to the letter.

Virgo displays this quiet, steely strength of character in other ways, too. They are unlikely to be swayed by false gods, unlikely to be so dazzled by fame or wealth or even love that they forget who they are and what they value. Virgo *knows*, deeply and with certainty, what is valuable and what is not, what is worthwhile and what is merely flashy.

This inner wisdom—knowing who one is, knowing right from wrong, knowing what is gold and what merely catches the sunlight—means Virgo is a sign capable of making important decisions quietly and without drama, without waffling, and with a clearheaded vision. Virgo is able to set a course without the need for affirmation or permission from others. Part of this confidence comes from the practicality of Virgo's nature, and some from a clear-eyed confidence in one's own wisdom. Virgo is able to cut through all unnecessary information to see the world, the situation, and the stakes clearly, and to react based on values, based on selfhood, based on what really matters.

So much of the time, what really matters is simply *showing up* to do what has to be done, and Virgo is a sign that shows up. In *Close to the Knives*, Wojnarowicz spends so much of his time in hospitals and at doctor's appointments with lovers and friends, but even before this—before AIDS started killing his friends while the American government watched and did nothing—his earlier diaries are full of moments, large and small, of showing up. He bails a friend out of jail. He goes with a friend to get an IUD implanted. ("I thought of how terrible it is that women undergo this sort of shit for men.") He drives out to New Jersey to pick up a friend who needs him. He gives a friend a jar of his urine so that the friend won't get kicked out of his methadone program.

Beyond the world of the novel, Leslie Feinberg, too, showed hirself over and over again to be personally willing to show up for other people, not only in hir writing (both in hir book and in journalism for *Workers World*) but also in organizing and activism in solidarity with the poor and working classes, people of color, and Palestinians. After getting the rights back to *Stone Butch Blues,* Feinberg decided to take it "off the capitalist market" and not seek a new commercial publishing contract, instead making it available for free on hir website. "I give this novel back to the workers and oppressed of the world." Even as ze was undergoing treatment for the cancer that would eventually kill hir, ze worked hard to organize and advocate for CeCe McDonald, the black trans woman arrested in Minneapolis in 2011 for defending herself after being attacked by a group of older white people. Feinberg tagged the wall of the county jail with spray paint: FREE CECE NOW! "As a journalist," ze wrote, "author, and proud member of the National Writers Union/UAW 1981—I'm most proud of writing those three words."

Looked at in this way, it's easy to see how Virgo's perfectionism doesn't have to be something limited, focused only on the self, focused only on establishing absolute personal control. Virgo isn't only a Virgo in the contained environment of the house, the kitchen, the office. Virgo is still Virgo when looking out into the vast, chaotic world. Virgo is still Virgo even when the world's anarchic wrongness is too great to be tamed.

It's simple enough to notice the ways Virgo strives to bring order to the space of a private, personal life. But what does Virgo energy look like when it's released onto a tangled world? If the archetypal Virgo image is a woman carrying a tall sheaf of wheat—if Virgo is the sign of the harvest—what happens when the harvest is poisoned? What happens when the fields yield not sheaves of golden wheat but soil ruined by pesticides and over-farming, or buckets of rotting fruit?

Virgo gets enough credit for its courage to keep living in a world that can't be controlled, no matter how hard Virgo tries. What does striving for order look like in an irredeemably chaotic world? What could striving for perfection look like in a world that keeps betraying you, over and over again?

If order is the thing that matters most, and if it's also the thing that's not possible, what is left for Virgo to do?

What's left to do is bear witness, by which I mean looking at reality with a resolute strength, without flinching: to record the truth of the world without lying, without softening, without sugarcoating, but with love.

THIS IS WHERE VIRGO'S RULING planet, Mercury, comes in. Mercury is the planet of knowledge and language, of communication, the planet of connection with other people. It's the "with other people" part that's crucial here. Virgo can project an energy of receptive quietness, of internal solidity, and this can make us forget that Virgo is also, fundamentally, a sign about connection. Virgo's knowledge, and its language, is rooted in the realities of the world.

In *Stone Butch Blues*, gender-nonconforming characters are assaulted and beaten—sometimes by the police and sometimes by regular civilian homophobes—with regularity. Some of them die. Some of them vanish. One is institutionalized, retreating so far inside herself that she stops speaking. "How had Al survived?" Jess realizes while visiting. "By forgetting, going to sleep, going away! She went underground, hid for safety." While it's a novel, it's the type of novel that had readers constantly asking Feinberg whether or not it was "true," whether the events described really happened. "Oh, it's real all right. So real it bleeds," Feinberg wrote in 2003. A document of a real time, a real world. A document bearing witness to a real history.

David Wojnarowicz learned he was HIV positive in 1987. He died in 1992. While he was writing, it was from the position of a person in the center of an epidemic, a crisis and a tragedy of such proportions that there was no way for one person to turn it into something orderly, something clear, something just.

Bringing this into a project about astrology at all feels a little bit sacrilegious, as though I'm blithely trying to climb Everest in my cheap parka from H&M, as though I'm cheerfully throwing a birthday party in a haunted house. This kind of pop astrology, the kind I've been writing, is supposed to be *fun*, I can imagine you may be thinking; it's supposed to be memes and games and lightness; it's supposed to be contained and personal. It's supposed to support the idea that we can compartmentalize our higher, enduring selves from the worlds we live in. As though astrology only works in the good times. As though astrology can only be applicable to the safest and least vulnerable among us. If astrology's going to be worth anything, it needs to have something to offer us, even when the world is awful, and even when that awfulness permeates every last space in our lives.

AT ITS BEST, VIRGO'S ENERGY is not about compressing life into a small, dead, perfect object. It's not about the endpoint—not about actually possessing perfection—but about making everyday choices with care and attention to what matters. It's about the undying hope for a better world than the one we live in now. Virgo can be critical and demanding, not because Virgo hates the world, but because Virgo is brave enough to believe it could be better. This isn't a position of fussiness but of a courageous and vulnerable idealism. Virgo's great wisdom, its great gift to us, is loving the world enough to believe that it can be better than it is now.

There's a difference between loving a bright amorphous "future" and loving the world, the existing world, enough to want to see it change. This underlying sense of responsibility and care—both as a thing that one can feel and a value that one can enact—is what shines brightest in Virgo. And it's what gets lost sometimes when we talk about Virgo as merely an organizer of sock drawers. Virgo's capacity to bear unflinching witness isn't limited to the personal, to the interpersonal, to the domestic. Virgo can keep an orderly kitchen, but Virgo can also look out in the world and stand under the full, crushing weight of its injustices.

Virgo is a sign with a powerful desire for the world to be orderly, just, humane. If the world were orderly and just and humane, maybe Virgo would be defined by those more finicky, perfectionist tendencies. But Virgo lives, as we all do, in the world that actually exists, and that means that Virgo, like all of us, must contend with powerful forces arrayed against the very possibility of a small and orderly life. In the real world, sometimes "orderliness" becomes impossible. Sometimes "orderliness"—quiet, calm, structure, peace—becomes a cudgel in the hands of those in power. This is the Reagan administration's utter failure to act on, or even acknowledge, the AIDS crisis. This is the so-called moral majority's insistence on creating an "orderly" society in which gay people aren't seen, in which they die in an epidemic, in which they don't exist at all. It's the police in Jess Goldberg's Buffalo, New York, creating "order" by raiding the gay bars and assaulting the patrons with a sickening, brutal regularity.

But Virgo's orderliness—its steadiness, its focus on detail, its clear and unwavering gaze on the workings of the world—is not a tool of repression. It's not a mechanism for tamping down the world's bright diversity or its anarchic energy, nor a tool for shutting out the bigger picture, nor a means of preventing the world from blossoming, from growing, from changing in big ways. Leslie Feinberg's obituary in the *Advocate* reported that hir final words were "Remember me as a revolutionary communist," spoken after a long life of loving and fighting and showing up to do the work. It seems, at first glance, distinctly un-Virgo: big, bold, confrontational. But why shouldn't Virgo be all these things? The order Virgo wants most is somewhere far in the distance, and it's loving, it's bright, it holds room for everyone, and if Virgo has to travel through some chaos to get there, they'll do it. They'll show up.

LIBRA

The Celebrity

IN 2018, DURING THE FIRST WEEK OF LIBRA SEASON, TMZ REPORTED THAT THE RAPPER CARDI B, A LIBRA, "TURNED HERSELF IN" TO THE POLICE AFTER "ORDERING AN ATTACK" ON TWO BARTENDERS AT A QUEENS STRIP CLUB. The language is sensational enough to give the whole incident a sinister shimmer of mob-adjacent high drama—*ordered an attack!* But later in the story another source described it as something closer to a bar fight—spontaneous and chaotic—than a mob hit. Cardi suspected one of the bartenders of having slept with her husband, the rapper Offset, and she and her group threw bottles, chairs, and "a hookah smoking device."

The fight itself seems decidedly un-Libra-like. Libra is known for its diplomatic nature, its general equanimity, its values of harmony, balance, and tact; it's not one of the more likely candidates for starting a brawl in the club. Circumstances can sometimes push even the most classic, most self-possessed of Libras too far. Still, the fight itself seems more likely a manifestation of other placements in Cardi's chart—her aggressive Aries moon, maybe, or her intense and jealous Scorpio Mercury and Venus.

Nonetheless, the real Libra energy came through in full force later when Cardi reported (or "turned herself in," per TMZ) to the police, and all the gossip sites ran photos of her leaving the precinct. In these photos she looked for all the world like a celebrity on a press tour, like a beautiful visiting dignitary, like a beloved and precious national hero come to shine down on her fans. Without context, it looked like she was there for some kind of utterly benign PR engagement. Even with the context, the photos gave the impression that everyone there was so dazzled by her charm that they forgot their jobs, that they were just there to bask in her light, to get an autograph and see her smile. The police who escorted her out of the building looked practically like her staff; dressed in drab and competent blue, they offered a background against which Cardi shone. She was an absolute vision in the photos, dressed in a sexy-professional outfit reminiscent of something Elle Woods would wear to court in *Legally Blonde*—a crisp, tan jacket over a radiantly white ruffled blouse, a beige midi-skirt that hit below the knees but had slits all the way to the tops of her thighs. Her chin-length, white-blond bob looked like movie-star hair, and she waved like the queen: charming, bright, unbothered. This wasn't a perp walk by any stretch of the imagination.

These were photos of a charm about as Libran as it gets. This charm was not the glittering and insubstantial thing we sometimes mean when we use the word, nor was it the slick and vaguely unsettling tactic of a salesperson trying to weasel their way into your wallet. Rather, like all the best Libra charm, it reflected a real-world, real-life magic. It transformed a police summons into something that looked very much like a triumph. It continues to allow Cardi B to move through the world—from stripper to viral Instagram star to

Love & Hip-Hop: New York star to certified platinum Grammy winner—and cross every barrier designed to keep her out, smiling a movie-star smile while she does it.

LIBRA CHARM ISN'T THE ENGINE that initially drives a person into the public eye, but once they've arrived, it might be the thing that makes the rest of us want to keep gazing. Libra charm can seemingly neutralize all obstacles, not through force but through beauty and persuasion. Libra is, in many ways, the sign of the capital-C Celebrity: it hardly matters what specifically they're famous for. What matters is their particular airy sparkle, their luxurious grace in front of all the world's attention.

Cardi B, for example, is famous as a rapper; she's the first female solo rapper to have a number one single in more than twenty years. And she's *good* at what she does. The Libra celebrity quality, however, comes from somewhere else. She's eminently charismatic, watchable, delightful, whether she's giving an interview or descending the steps of a police precinct station or telling a joke on Instagram.

Gwyneth Paltrow, a Libra, first became famous as an actor, notably in highbrow period pieces like *Emma*, *Great Expectations*, and *Shakespeare in Love*, but appearing, too, in blockbuster comedies (*Shallow Hal*, a cameo in *Austin Powers in Goldmember*), romances (*Possession, Bounce*), and Wes Anderson's *Royal Tenenbaums*. Between 1991 and 2019 she's appeared in at least one movie nearly every year. Yet, at this point, as a cultural figure, she sparks brightest not for her movies but for her sheer Gwyneth-ness, her essence itself. She appears in the news for noteworthy developments in her personal life—her "conscious uncoupling" from Chris Martin; the revelation that she and current husband, Brad Falchuk, live together only part-time—and for the outlandish "wellness" advice offered by her Goop brand. "Is Gwyneth Paltrow just kind of strange or is she a visionary?" asked Sunny Hostin on *The View*. It hardly matters, just as it hardly matters whether she keeps starring in movies or not; her air of celebrity keeps us watching either way.

And Kim Kardashian, a Libra, has seemed to accrue fame as though she's a powerful magnet, drawing our attention toward her regardless of what precisely it is she is doing. In a 2019 conversation in *Interview* magazine, Hari Nef—also a Libra—asked Courtney Love to "describe the ideal woman." Love answered that she has become "really ensorcelled" (!) by "this Venusian fertility cult in the Valley"—the Valley being the San Fernando, and the fertility cult being, of course, the Kardashians.

"ENSORCELLING" IS A NOT-INCORRECT WORD for what it is that a powerful Libra energy can do to us. And Love's naming of the Venusian vibe of it all is an unintentionally astute astrological observation, too.

Venus—planet of sensuality, beauty, luxury, love—is the ruling planet of Libra. Venus is the second brightest object in our night sky. In the right conditions, it's bright enough to be visible in broad daylight; at its brightest, it can cast delicate shadows on earth. It has a heavy, sulfurous atmosphere that would be unbreathable to humans, but from here on earth, that atmosphere just looks beautiful—soft and creamy and lush. Where Mercury is cratered and Mars is rocky, Venus looks like luxury itself—like foamed milk, like cream-colored silk, like clouds above the horizon.

Certain (mostly outdated) conventions in astrology maintain that your sign can determine how you look: Linda Goodman wrote in her classic book *Sun Signs* that Libran features are "almost always even and well-balanced," they almost always have dimples, their hair is often curly, and "you'll never meet a Libran who doesn't have a smile like a soft, white cloud." I've read elsewhere that Libra comes with a "dulcet voice," "small but pretty hands," or "heart-shaped lips." According to this line of thinking, Libras are likely to be particularly lovely, with particularly symmetrical faces—just like celebrities! This has always struck me as improbable, but even without believing that Libra must be personally beautiful, it's easy to see the ways Libra is *drawn* toward beauty, whether that means making themselves beautiful or seeking out and appreciating beauty in the world.

Gwyneth's whole Goop empire is a good example: although it's ostensibly a "wellness" business, Gwyneth's is a vision of wellness founded in lovely things. Gwyneth sells us beautiful things as a way to sell a dream of a beautiful, balanced, healthy life. For her, luxury isn't incidental to wellness, but a central part of it.

She told a classroom of business students, reported Taffy Brodesser-Akner in the *New York Times*, that it was "crucial to me that we remain aspirational . . . The ingredients are beautiful. You can't get that at a lower price point. You can't make these things mass-market."

She continually comes under fire for this attitude, charged with being elitist or out of touch, but it is emblematic of classic Libran values. For Libra, beauty and luxury are worthy goals to strive for. It isn't about reaching for the *status* that comes from having a closet full of cashmere and silk, for example, it's about the luxury and the pleasure to be found in the objects themselves.

Cardi B's Venusian ethic is equally luxurious: the thick eyelashes, the long acrylics, the Louboutin red bottoms she sings about in "Bodak Yellow." At the 2019 Met Gala, she wore a dress made of 30,000 feathers; it reportedly took 2,000 hours to make. And, wearing it, Cardi gave the impression of being thrilled and enchanted by her own glamour, by the luxury she has access to. Libra is not, for the most part, interested in consuming conspicuously or dazzling other people with excess; if anything, Libras wants to perform for and delight themselves.

Even Kim Kardashian, whose sexiness is intensely performative, tends to give the impression that she's performing for herself, too. She seems like a person as fully entranced by the miracle of her beauty as we are, as much in awe as anyone else of the magic properties of nature and science that made her look this way.

This can look like vanity, sure, but I think it's something different. In *Ways of Seeing*, John Berger famously defended the woman caught enjoying her own reflection: "You painted a naked woman because you enjoyed looking at her, put a mirror in her hand and you called the painting 'Vanity,' thus morally condemning the woman whose nakedness you had depicted for your own pleasure." To take it a step farther: Would it be so bad if she *were* admiring herself in the mirror? Would it be such a scandal if she *did* simply appreciate the beauty of her own face, her own shape, her own life? Is she not allowed that?

THIS VENUSIAN INFLUENCE AND LOVE of beauty can lead to Libra being taken less seriously than it really deserves. Indeed, the very comparison of Libra with celebrity can sound laughably unserious. When I was a teenager, the adults in my life—my parents, my friends' parents, the teachers I loved best at school—talked as though there was no worse thing to be than a celebrity. This wasn't a criticism of the whole unhealthy ecosystem of fame so much as it was a criticism of the actual people themselves: vain and useless, probably stupid, "famous for being famous." These people—nearly always women—were presented as contagions of a cultural epidemic of superficiality, vanity, moral weakness.

Some years later, smartphones would be widely adopted and selfies would draw some of this moralizing fire. But at the time, the focus was on the celebrity. This was the era of early reality TV: the first season of *The Bachelor* (2002); *The Simple Life* (2003) with Paris Hilton and Nicole Richie; *Laguna Beach* (2004); *The Hills* (2006); the birth of the *Real Housewives* franchise (*The Real Housewives of Orange County*, 2006). Audiences watched people on these shows spending their time making themselves beautiful and striving toward love and enjoying the things their money could buy. This seemed simply unconscionable to people like my English teacher who posted a sign that said NO FRIVOLITY on the classroom wall, or my best friend's mother who once rented a grainy VHS copy of a dry-as-sawdust biopic of Sir Thomas More for us to watch on a sleepover.

The fear was, I think, that we—the middle-class white teenage girls of my town—would be seduced by glimmering, glamorous surfaces, and we'd forget our own depths, our own capacity for hard work and discipline. It wasn't exactly a fear that we'd grow up to be unsuccessful: in seemingly all levels of white culture, after all, from Paris Hilton to then president George W. Bush (who is, by the way, a Libra moon), frivolous charmers were constantly being rewarded. The fear, instead, was that these bad role models, these Pied Pipers of wealth and charm, would lead us toward success but away from everything solid and serious and good in the world, leaving us, in the end, with nothing: no inner life, no moral center, no respect for hard work or our principles. All our successes would be hollow, meaningless, built on nothing but air.

BUT AS LIBRA, AN AIR sign, can show us, air isn't a negligible thing. These are the signs not just of sociability and charm but also of intellect, of curiosity, of the life of the mind. Their airiness can make them, on one hand, less grounded than some of the other signs, but it can also make them freer to wander, freer to ask broad questions, freer to observe the world with a heart that's curious, not defensive. In our colloquial speech, "airiness" can connote some kind of spacey unseriousness, but the air signs in astrology can let us see something entirely different instead. Air signs can have thoughts that move so fast, they're nearly impossible to see. Air signs can have thoughts that exist on an altogether different, heightened plane.

I don't entirely blame the grown-ups for their anxiety about our futures: much of the culture *did* elevate wealth and appearances over all else. But everything got tangled up, so that pleasure and beauty and charm, generally speaking, became objects of some suspicion. To value beauty at all was to risk emptying out your entire soul.

Using the sign of Libra as a lens can offer a way to separate the two, to clear our heads of some of the moralistic cultural baggage that keeps clogging up our mental works. An orientation toward comfort or beauty isn't indicative of moral degeneracy, and sober asceticism is not a prerequisite for being smart or interesting or good! Libra offers a way to see how beauty and seriousness can exist in the same person, how sensuality and a deep care for the world can exist side by side, not in tension but in understanding with each other.

Indeed, it's useless to try to resist any one of the signs. All twelve signs will act on you throughout your life, and all twelve are represented somewhere in your chart, either through planets or house placements. This means that everyone, even my would-be Victorian governess of an English teacher, has some Libra energy inside them. You don't have to *love* every sign equally; just recognize that each one has an equal capacity for good and for evil, an equal capacity to ruin the world and to save it. And to reject out of hand a sign's broad energy is to cut yourself off from a part of your own multitudinous humanity. To believe that Libra energy is a harbinger of doom is to remove yourself from a powerful source of vitality, of balance, of valuable joy.

I'm arguing here that Libra gives us the opportunity to imagine charm as a true and valuable and valid form of magic. This is "charm" more like a spell. It's "charm" as a form of real power. And not just that, but a source of pure, bright delight. Even more, a source of delight with the power to make the world better.

LIBRA'S ENERGY IS NOT ALL focused on the self, but, rather, it looks outward, into the social world. While its air sign cousin Gemini can be, if highly social, also a little chaotic, Libra's air sign energy tends more toward the balanced, the tactful, the diplomatic. Libra places a high value on fairness, balance, and maintaining harmonious relationships with other people. If Gemini is the party guest who holds everyone's attention, Libra is the perfect host who makes you feel at ease no matter who else you know at the party, no matter how anxious parties make you feel. Even those of us who pride ourselves on "seeing through" charm, or being otherwise immune to it, can be absolutely susceptible when a Libra is the one doing the charming. This is because, in its truest form, Libra charm is not a tool to elicit a reaction, not a strategy to make its receiver do something, not a gambit to make the charmer seem special or trustworthy or likable. Libra knows, deeply and instinctively, how to treat other people with genuine interest and kindness, and considers this to be work worth doing.

This tendency toward harmony is represented in Libra's symbol, the scales, an image representative of Libra's values (balance, harmony, fairness) and also its skills (tact, equanimity, objectivity). Beyond Libra's ability to create harmonious social situations, Libra is also able to live in a place of intellectual objectivity, able to see a matter from all sides, to consider all parts of a situation with seriousness and care. After a breakup or a fight or a schism in a social group, Libra is most likely to manage the delicate balancing act of staying loyal and loving to all parties.

But Libra's instinctual inclination toward harmony can create difficulties, too. Of all the signs of the zodiac, Libra is the only one represented by an inanimate object, and its eternal balance can make it difficult for a Libra to move, to make decisions, to *act*. Libra can end up so concerned about seeing all sides of an issue that it becomes impossible to remember, or even to discover in the first place, what their *own* side really is. This doesn't mean that Libra can't make big choices. Once a Libra finally *does* take a stand, it's typically well considered, unwavering, and fair. What's more, they have the rare and miraculous gift of making their vision of fairness look not just beautiful but *charming*, reasonable, utterly correct.

Cardi B does it on social media constantly. She's talked about how much she loves FDR because of the New Deal and Social Security. She's tweeted in support of debt-ridden NYC cabdrivers. During the 2018–2019 government shutdown—the longest US government shutdown in history—she got on Instagram, animated and beautiful in peacock-green eyeshadow and long pink nails. As reported by *Slate*, she begins: "Hey y'all. I just want to remind you because it's been a bit over three weeks, okay? . . . Trump is now ordering, as in summonsing, federal government workers to go back to work without getting paid." She smartly anticipates that viewers might argue that there was a government shutdown under Obama, too, and lightly deflects it: "*Yeah*, bitch, for *health care*!

So your grandma could check her blood pressure and you bitches can go check your pussy at the gynecologist with no motherfuckin' problem!" She makes an argument for why her viewers should care: "Now, I know a lot of y'all don't care because y'all don't work for the government, or y'all probably don't even have a job, but this shit is really fucking serious, bro. This shit is crazy. Like, our country is in a hellhole right now. All for a fucking wall." And she ends with an expression of empathy and an admittedly vague call to action: "And we really need to take this serious—I feel like we need to take some action. I don't know what type of action, bitch, because this is not what I do. But bitch, I'm scared. This is crazy. And I really feel bad for these people that gotta go to fucking work to not get motherfucking paid."

It echoes the speech Alicia Silverstone—also a Libra—gave as Cher Horowitz in *Clueless*. In debate class, Cher and her social rival, Amber, face off at two lecterns at the front of the classroom. Their topic: "Should all oppressed people be allowed refuge in America?"

Amber has been assigned to argue against refuge; Cher, for it. Cher, dressed in her iconic yellow plaid miniskirt suit, is up first.

"So, okay," she says, smiling beatifically at her classmates, "like, right now, for example, the Haitians"—she pronounces this with three syllables, "Hai-ti-ans"—"need to come to America. But some people are all, what about the strain on our resources? But it's, like, when I had this garden party for my father's birthday, right, I said RSVP, because it was a sit-down dinner. But people came that, like, did not RSVP. So I was, like, totally bugging. I had to haul ass to the kitchen, redistribute the food, squish in extra place settings . . . but by the end of the day it was, like, the more, the merrier. And so, if the government could just get to the kitchen, rearrange some things, we could certainly party with the Haitians. And in conclusion, may I please remind you that it does *not* say RSVP on the Statue of Liberty!" The teacher leans back on his desk looking confused and disturbed, but Cher's classmates—who have been fidgeting, whispering, writing notes, painting their nails throughout the speech—greet this conclusion with applause and a hearty cheer.

Both speeches are by beautiful, heavily made-up women, speaking in a vernacular (Cardi's "y'all motherfuckers" and "fucking serious, bro"; Cher's "totally bugging" and "haul ass") precisely matched to their audiences, which would nonetheless have had my anti-frivolity English teacher tearing her hair out and calling the guidance counselor. Both speakers are disturbed by the presence of unfairness in the world. Both speeches are engaging, fun to watch, and both, in their own strange way, can make justice seem like the most reasonable and lovely of all the world's options.

IF YOU'RE WILLING NOT TO ask too many questions, it can look like the warnings of all those high school teachers turned out to be right about celebrity culture's toxic strangle-hold on our society. After the reality shows came Facebook and Instagram, selfies, the age of the influencer. The *Real Housewives* franchise is a venerable institution with nine domestic and ten international shows, and *Keeping Up with the Kardashians* aired its sixteenth season in 2019. Beyond the show, the Kardashians reign over a weird and sprawling empire of entertainment properties, cosmetics brands, and our public imagination. And still, the consequences of these Libra-inflected millennial values ended up being so much more surprising, and so much less catastrophic, than my poor alarmist teachers would have guessed.

Kim Kardashian—along with a team of lawyers and advocates—made a point of meeting with the president to discuss the case of Alice Marie Johnson, a sixty-three-year-old sentenced to life in prison, without the chance for parole, for a nonviolent drug offense. After their meeting, the president granted clemency to Johnson, who had been in prison for twenty-one years. In a profile for *Vogue*, Kardashian described feeling out of her depth in this meeting, surrounded by people who had been doing this work for many years. According to Kardashian and activist Van Jones, her role in the meeting was to use diplomacy and emotional intelligence to discuss "the human side" of the injustice of prisons in the United States, but she found herself wanting to know more, to be able to back up her opinions with facts. As Cardi said, someone needed to do something, but "I don't know what type of action, bitch, because this is not what I do." "If I knew more, I could do more," Kim Kardashian said, so she embarked on a plan to become a lawyer by completing a four-year law internship. At least, this is the story she tells. Kim Kardashian West isn't about to stop using her celebrity to sell makeup on Instagram, but she's doing some surprising things with her charm, too.

WHEN ALEXANDRIA OCASIO-CORTEZ, A LIBRA, was elected to Congress, pundits on the right and the center-left groused and griped that she was politically shallow and hadn't yet paid her dues, that she was simply pretty and nothing more, that she was operating according to some model of celebrity politics rather than something duller and stodgier. She may have *charm*, their complaints went, but does she have what it really takes?

This is the wrong question entirely to ask about a Libra, for whom charm isn't a distraction or a cover but a hidden power. Yes, she has charm, and it's a valuable tool indeed. Libra energy might not have been the thing that powered Ocasio-Cortez to canvass up and down Queens and the Bronx, but it was the quality that made people want to pay attention to her, and that made her constituents feel like they were being heard, like they were being seen. It's Libra energy that can keep people tuning into social media to watch a politician cook dinner and talk about socialism. We don't, after all, have to turn away from what makes us bright. We don't have to turn away from what makes us beautiful and charming. A wide smile and a pair of hoop earrings can hold just as much power as a raised fist.

SCORPIO

The Punk

THE SCENE: IT'S SCORPIO SEASON 2004, AND TO THE DELIGHT AND ANXIETY OF SEEMINGLY EVERYONE IN MY HOMETOWN IN NEW HAMPSHIRE, THE BOSTON RED SOX HAVE MADE IT TO THE WORLD SERIES. This will, eventually, be the year that the Red Sox finally break the curse that has purportedly kept them from winning a World Series since trading Babe Ruth to the Yankees in 1918, but nobody knows that yet. For now, there's just a buzz of anticipation in the air. The hallways at school are filled with kids in full Sox gear; strangers talk about it in restaurants and stores; the local paper runs frenzied human interest stories about sick and elderly people hanging on to life by the frayed thread of hope that they'll finally see Boston win.

But not me. I'm sixteen, equal parts pretentious and insecure, and I know that I don't *ever* want to reach the end of my life and have no passion more powerful than my love for a sports team. It has only been a few years since I started to really learn how blithely people in authority are willing to lie to themselves and each other. The Iraq war, at this point, is only a year and a half old, and what seems to me to be clearly, undeniably *wrong* is being neutralized and normalized, glossed over with yellow ribbon car magnets and SUPPORT OUR TROOPS signs, even in the basically liberal city where I live. Patriotism feels newly poisonous, and I have a sense that if only I can find it, the world holds something sharp and true and much more real than this. Nobody around me seems to have anything approaching an answer, but the people who appear at least to have a methodology for looking for one are the artists, the rebels, the punks.

So on the night of Game 1 of the 2004 World Series—Red Sox versus Cardinals at Fenway Park—my friends and I are in Boston, too. Not to see the baseball game but to see our most beloved electropunk band Le Tigre play a show at a venue that is, as we learn when we arrive, located directly behind Fenway Park. From the top of the street, where our friend's dad drops us off, the crowd splits neatly into two visually distinct streams of people. On the right, walking toward Fenway, are the Boston sports fans in red and navy Sox clothes, loud and drunk, among the most cartoonishly terrifying of America's jocks. On the left, a thinner stream of people—in combat boots and asymmetrical haircuts, fishnet tights and ragged denim jackets—moves toward the show, and we slip in among them.

Under the stadium lights across the street, the sports-goers will soon hear Steven Tyler perform the national anthem. In the dark club, we will hear Kathleen Hanna, a Scorpio, insult President George W. Bush and sing a song calling New York City mayor Rudy Giuliani "such a fuckin' jerk," and my heart will swell with the feeling that at last, an adult is telling me the truth about the world. Not just the literal truth—plenty of adults in my life also believed the war was wrong and the president's policies were bad—but the angry emotional truth of it, too. This war is wrong, and the people in power don't care about you, and Giuliani is such a fucking jerk.

While there's nothing exactly radical about being a white sixteen-year-old yelling with her friends in a concert venue rather than in a baseball stadium—although at the time I thought there probably was—punk shows still opened a door to a depth and provocative courage I might never have found anywhere else. Punk singers like Kathleen Hanna modeled what it could look like to get angry at the state of the world, and to take control of that anger, and use it to tell the truth.

SCORPIO OCCUPIES A PLACE IN the zodiac similar to the space punk occupies in the music world, and I don't say that just because I went to one Le Tigre show. Both offer provocation and secrets and sharp edges, a willingness to disturb the peace. At their very best, both offer an intensity that refuses superficiality and refuses to be placated by appearances. Both offer the courage to look directly into the world's darkness and not run from what is found there. While Libra, immediately before Scorpio in the zodiac, tends to seek out beauty and justice, Scorpio's vision is often pulled in the opposite direction: toward the ways the world is *unfair*; toward sites of ugliness and suffering.

But for Scorpio, awareness of the world's cruelty and darkness doesn't have to lead to fear or anger necessarily. If uncertainty and the unknown are what make us most afraid—the reason why horror movies reveal their monsters only in haunting, fleeting glimpses—Scorpio deals with fear not by avoiding the unknown, but by seeking it out, by spending so much time in the world's dark places that those places become familiar. Scorpio is willing to seek out the world's monsters, and stare at them head-on. Scorpio believes that evil exists, but isn't afraid. If anyone has the fortitude—and also the desire—to plumb the depths of the world's darkness and reemerge to speak about it, unintimidated and true, it's Scorpio. Or it's a punk. Or both.

Kathleen Hanna of Bikini Kill and Le Tigre has three planets in Scorpio, including the sun. Alice Bag of the Bags has four. Corin Tucker of Sleater-Kinney, Laura Jane Grace of Against Me!, and Nadezhda Tolokonnikova of Pussy Riot have Scorpio suns, too. (The Yeah Yeah Yeahs' Karen O, a Scorpio, is not strictly speaking a punk, but try to watch that "Maps" video—dark eyeliner, sweaty hair in her eyes, that deep burning gaze—and tell me she's not among the very punkest in the indie rock world of the 2000s.)

SCORPIO IS THE FIRST OF three signs (the others are Aquarius and Pisces) with two different ruling planets, one ancient and one modern. Ancient astrologers recognized only seven planets, because they could only view as far in the sky as Saturn. With more zodiac signs than planets in the sky, some of the signs doubled up. Gemini and Virgo were both ruled by Mercury, and still are; Taurus and Libra by Venus. Aries and Scorpio—both confident, powerful, assured—were ruled by bold and driven Mars.

Then, in 1930, American astronomer Clyde Tombaugh discovered the ninth planet, Pluto. The new planet's name was credited to Venetia Burney, age eleven, who loved classical mythology and thought the god of the underworld was a fitting namesake for this mysterious, dark, faraway planet. In addition to being lonely and far away, Pluto's orbit is both eccentric—meaning that it's elliptical, rather than circular—and chaotic, meaning that it's so sensitive to small changes and disturbances in the solar system that scientists can't predict its long-term path.

When a new planet is discovered and named, astrology understands it to reflect a new archetypal force coming into cultural prominence, a new cosmic theme entering our understanding of humanity. Pluto, which was discovered as the Great Depression was beginning and as European fascism was ascending, and just before Otto Hahn discovered nuclear fission, is associated with forces of transformation, destruction, and rebirth, and the powers that live beneath the surface. It seemed only natural that this newly discovered dark planet would be linked to Scorpio, the sign of human darkness and depth.

Like Pluto, Scorpio has an energy that is dark and strange and bendy, both eccentric and chaotic. This is the energy of turning over a rock in the forest to see what lives underneath; it's the energy of diving to the bottom of the ocean to see what happens in the sea's near-total blackness. This is an energy pulled, as if magnetically, to the universe's spiritual and emotional depths. This is an energy that fears no darkness.

Before Pluto was discovered, though, Scorpio was understood to be ruled by aggressive Mars, and Mars remains crucially illustrative of the more straightforwardly powerful parts of Scorpio's energy: its boldness, its drive, its tendency to be unshrinking and provocative. In this way, Scorpio can be seen as the dark cousin of Aries, also ruled by Mars. Both signs can make for powerful personalities, both can be driven, both can be fearless. But if Aries is red and gold glitter, Scorpio is black glitter, reflecting light while at the same time absorbing it, hiding it, keeping it private inside itself. If Aries as a vocalist is the diva, then Scorpio as a vocalist is a punk. If Mars's influence on Aries sounds like Celine Dion's uncomplicated assurance when she sings, "Don't give up on your faith / Love comes to those who believe it / And that's the way it is," then its influence on Scorpio might sound more like Alice Bag yelling the lyrics "She's taken too much of the domesticated world, she's tearing it to pieces, she's a violence girl." Or like Laura Jane Grace of Against Me! singing in "FUCKMYLIFE666," "Don't wanna live without teeth / Don't wanna die without bite." Or like Kathleen Hanna: "I wanna burn, baby burn / Baby black and blue / Burn it baby burn it baby / Burn with the truth." This is Mars boldness combined with Pluto's dark edge, Mars's red heat threaded through with Pluto's goth undercurrents.

THIS DARK EDGE MEANS THAT Scorpio has traditionally been more strongly associated with sex than any other of the signs. While Scorpio's cousin Aries is associated with sex as pure animal instinct, and its polar opposite Taurus is associated with sex as pure sensuality, Scorpio is the sign associated with the pure, perverse, dangerous, skin-prickling *sexiness* of sex.

And just as sex has sometimes been viewed as something evil or unnatural, as a doorway to disturbing powers, Scorpio has also, historically, been seen as a bearer of dark powers. Scorpio's relation to sex collides with our continuing cultural anxieties about sex—not just sex itself, but the power of self-determination that it represents. For people who aren't straight and cisgender men, in particular, asserting our right to our pleasures and desires, to our sexual and reproductive freedom, is one way we assert our right to our own lives. Kathleen Hanna told the Rumpus, for instance, that when she got an abortion as a teenager, it was one of the best things that happened to her: "Not actually being on the table and having it done, but feeling like I was responsible for my own life and realizing that when I made mistakes, there were consequences and that I could take care of those consequences. I could make mistakes and I could fix them. And live with them." Scorpio understands that sexuality is a part of human existence, and controlling our own sexualities is crucial to controlling our own destinies.

And Scorpio understands, too, the powerful forces arrayed *against* people's right to control their own destinies, sexual and otherwise. More than maybe any other sign, Scorpio understands the movement of power through the world, suffering no illusions that the world operates solely according to principles of love or fairness. Scorpio doesn't imagine for even one second that the world abides by the official, stated rules; it understands that every last one of us operates within a framework of interlocking and conflicting modes of power, and we all need to learn to navigate these powers. Scorpio can show us how it's possible to threaten power, too: the power of the state, the power of the church, the power of the people who control the world's resources.

In order to challenge the existing powers in the world, it's necessary first to recognize it *as* power, to see it clearly. It's necessary to see an oppressive government *not* as a force as natural as the winds but rather as something that was built by people, and that's maintained by people, and that therefore can be disobeyed and resisted by people, too. Scorpio isn't evil; it's just willing to challenge all the powers that be.

And while it can be naïve to imagine that punk music by itself can cause these structures to come crashing down, punk can certainly be part of a larger ethos of rebellion. Pussy Riot,

for example—including Scorpio Nadezhda Tolokonnikova—
brought that ethos out from music venues and into the broader
world in 2012 when she and four others, including Maria Alyokhina and Yekaterina Samutsevich, stormed the Cathedral
of Christ the Saviour in Moscow dressed in neon and bala-
clavas to perform their song "Punk Prayer." "Our Lady," they
sang, "chase Putin out!" Church security stopped the performance after only about a minute. A little over a week later,
Tolokonnikova and Alyokhina were arrested and charged with
hooliganism; Samutsevich was arrested two weeks after that.
All three were denied bail and held for about five months until the trial, at which all three were convicted of "hooliganism
motivated by religious hatred" and sentenced to two years in
prison.

The prosecutors, the government, and most of the Russian media tried to cast Tolokonnikova and her comrades as
dark agents of evil and antireligious hatred; each woman, in
her statement to the court, affirmed again and again that the
target of their performance wasn't religious belief itself, but
the government, and the Russian Orthodox church's entangle-
ment with it. "We put on political punk performances," said
Tolokonnikova, "in response to a government that is rife with
rigidity, reticence, and caste-like hierarchal structures. It is so
clearly invested in serving only narrow corporate interests, it
makes us sick just to breathe the Russian air." Their project, as
each member of the group clearly stated more than once, was

to strike a blow at oppressive state power. The performance was powerful enough that the prosecution, Tolokonnikova said in her statement, had been forbidden from reading out their song's lyrics, or even speaking its title. "Despite the fact that we are physically here," she said, "we are freer than everyone sitting across from us on the side of the prosecution. We can say anything we want and we say everything we want." Through fearlessness and provocation, Scorpio can become free.

BUT SCORPIO'S WILLINGNESS TO PROVOKE and to tell frightening truths can lead to Scorpio being misunderstood by the rest of the zodiac and the rest of the world. Scorpios, like punks, can seem terrifying to people who don't *want* to deal with darkness or discord or intensity, who want a quiet, regular, mainstream life. Scorpios and punks can seem pointlessly, alarmingly antagonistic.

The apparent antagonism can make most people assume that Scorpio is a fire sign. But it's not; it's a water sign, and it shows us that water's elemental energy isn't melty, diluted, or weak. Although Scorpio may be the most intense flavor of water sign, it is still of a kind with its cousins Cancer and Pisces. These are the signs that can seep through surfaces, down into the depths. These are the signs with a finger on the underground beating pulse of feeling in the world. These are the signs most comfortable in true, abiding intimacy, and least comfortable with lightness and surfaces—the signs whose goal is closeness, intimacy, and feeling.

Likewise, Scorpio's punk ethos might make it sound as though Scorpio is a sign with a particularly loud personality— all the screaming, all the lace-up boots and middle fingers up, all the guitars so bright and distorted, you can hear them down the block. Knowing all this, it might seem weird or paradoxical or perversely contrarian to argue that Scorpio's *not* necessarily loud—but it's true. If anything, Scorpio's personality tends toward the reserved—the better to observe power as it flows and pools and accumulates, the better to maintain personal control. In 2019, Kathleen Hanna tweeted, in reference to women's history month, "Please stop tagging me as a rad woman for woman month. I am more creepy than brave."

This is a complicated relationship with stardom. No matter how loud Scorpio is at the punk show, no matter how bright and brazen, Scorpio's natural energy still tends more toward the DIY venue than the arena. As a water sign, a scorpion with an exoskeleton every bit as hard as Cancer's, Scorpio tends toward privacy, thriving in spaces where audiences are small and committed and in community with one another. Scorpio understands that too much visibility can lead to weakness; the punk world—a decentralized constellation of living rooms and basements, backyards and garages, warehouses and lofts—can manage and contain that visibility. Sometimes flyers for shows give up nothing at all: "Location: Ask a punk." It can offer something much closer to the intimacy and privacy, even secrecy, that Scorpio seeks.

In Alice Bag's memoir, *Violence Girl*, she opens with a description of a show she's playing. "I spot an area of spectators in front of Patricia, my bassist. Fuck that! No spectators, we're all participants here! I get up in their faces . . . Now they're dancing, that's right, keep it going." This is the provocative intimacy that Scorpio requires: *nobody* gets to hold themselves outside of it. Everyone's down here in the thick of things together, and Scorpio will get all the way up in your face to bring you into the thick of things, too. It's a refrain I've heard echoed again and again by performers at punk shows: "No voyeurs here." "Nobody's a spectator." If you're here, in other words, be ready to be *in it*.

This insistence on intimacy points to the fact that, in spite of everything, there *is* a softness to Scorpio, a vulnerability, an achy yearning underneath all the provocation, underneath all the slippery power games, underneath the aggressive and defensive posturing. Scorpio is still, after all, a water sign. Scorpio might hide every feeling, but that doesn't mean the feelings aren't there, deep and intense. And really, even when a punk singer screams their vocals—over deafeningly noisy guitars and drums—it isn't always a way to express aggression but can be a tactic for masking softness, too: a way to be heard without being heard too clearly, a way to make sure that the words themselves remain hidden beneath a layer of noise and distortion. Scorpio might act cynically—might *be* cynical—but it's less out of a belief that love or true friendship or a better world is impossible, and more from the certain knowledge, born of both observation and intuition, that this world we're living in right now isn't it. Scorpio wants a better world, a better life, purely and desperately, and Scorpio won't be convinced that something imperfect, violent, secondrate, is enough.

YEARS AFTER MY FIRST PUNK shows in New Hampshire and Boston, I was living in Brooklyn and feeling again like I was being lied to every day. This time it was at a demoralizing AmeriCorps job, where chipper program staffers repeated to us, again and again, that we were doing incredibly valuable work even though we were paid a stipend that, worked out hourly, hovered right below the minimum wage. The program repeated to us, again and again, that we were making New York City a better place, even though anyone could see that most of us spent our days sitting in desk chairs with nothing much to do, in a haze of dissatisfaction. It seemed unbelievable that there existed people willing to accept these clear untruths—that these working conditions were normal, acceptable, livable; that the work we did was making anyone's lives better—but there were.

And again, it was the punks in the program who offered a vision of something better—who showed up to our program meetings and asked why things were like this. It was the punks in the program who heckled the bank representative who tried to give us a presentation about saving our stipends to buy a house—us, making $6 an hour, save for a house? It was the punks who weren't willing to shut up about how useless the whole thing was.

Outside of work, too, it was the punks who moved like they knew the world's darkness and could face it bravely, laughing. It was the punks who moved through the world like they knew a secret, like they bore unusual powers. And it was the punk shows where, if somebody shoved you, if somebody disrespected your space, you got to shove back. Shoving back, and relentlessly telling the truth about the badness of things as they were, is a way of insisting that things don't *have* to be this way and things *won't always* be this way. It's a way to keep alive the possibility of something better.

It's such a Scorpio way to view the world—that, underneath the world's polished surface, there's something else, darker and rougher but glittering and alive. Underneath all the cheery encouraging words, underneath the demands of office decorum, underneath the world in which we're all expected to value comfort and stability and money, there are other truths to be found and other ways to relate to ourselves and each other. Scorpio can show us that it's possible to value the depth more than the surface, the truth more than the appearance. This Scorpio ethos is a model of fearlessness in the face of power. It's a model of being unmoved by intimidation and unafraid to see the truth about a world or a scene or a system that's rotten.

But in the end, this Scorpio fearlessness isn't the same as hardness, as much as Scorpios may try to make it look that way. Scorpio's willingness to enter the darkness can be an act of tremendous vulnerability and faith, based not on blithe optimism but on an aching desire to believe that no matter how dangerous things get in the dark, it would be infinitely worse to settle for a life that is safe but dishonest. It's a desire to believe that, through all the darkness, on the other side, there's something truly good waiting to be found.

THAT NIGHT IN BOSTON AT the Le Tigre show, before I knew who I was and before I knew what choices were available to me, their songs opened a doorway, just a crack, to show me a vision of what a life might look like where people told the truth. A vision of what life might look like if I, too, got so fed up by the things I saw happening in the world that I stood up on a stage and screamed about it. To my young and small and naïve self, Kathleen Hanna, a Scorpio, was a role model: somebody fully aware of all the shadows in the world, and choosing to live anyway as though she was unafraid.

But there was one song they played that flat out made me cry—that makes me cry still every time I put it on. It's the last track on Le Tigre's 1999 self-titled album, and unlike other songs on that album, it retains none of Bikini Kill's noisy, frenetic energy. This one is mid-tempo, simultaneously bouncy and plaintive, sung not shouted. Kathleen Hanna sings to her childhood neighbors Les and Ray, thanking them for being there—really, just for existing near her—when she was young. "I put my head up against the wall / To be closer to the music that they played," she sings, and my heart thumps out of my chest for this child feeling some kind of love or recognition when she looked at her neighbors, and seeing in that a tiny chance that the world might hold something better for her.

Every so often I'll hear an old Le Tigre song, usually in a bar or at a party, but only the throwback bangers, never this one. This one's the hidden side of Scorpio—the Scorpio who still waits for that tiny crack of light, hoping for more, wanting to believe in change, wanting to think there could ever be something better than this.

SAGITTARIUS

The Alter Ego

FIRST THERE WAS DESTINY HOPE CYRUS, A SAG-ITTARIUS, BORN NOVEMBER 1992. Then Destiny Hope Cyrus became Miley Ray Cyrus, and then Miley Ray Cyrus became Miley Ray Stewart, main character of the Disney Channel sitcom *Hannah Montana*. Her Disney Channel character is a teen with a double life: by day she's just Miley, going to school, dealing with friendships and crushes, engaging in social combat with mean and exclusionary popular girls. By night she disguises herself with wigs and sunglasses and becomes Hannah Montana, universally beloved pop megastar.

Miley wants to keep her second identity a secret from her friends and classmates, fearing that if they were to find out, they'd only be able to think of her as a celebrity, no longer simply a friend. Revealing her other identity would smooth the way for her in many ways—everyone, even the popular girls, would treat her with instant adoration—but this isn't worth it. She doesn't want to be recognized, surveilled, attended to everywhere she goes; she doesn't want her stardom to foreclose the possibility of a normal, non-famous, regular-girl life. She values her regular-girlness and the space it offers her for curiosity, for exploration, for learning about the world as it really is, not the world as it is for the famous. Crucially, though, she doesn't value her regular-girlness so much that she's willing to give up her pop star self, and much of the

show's drama lives in this tension: in Miley's desire to pro-
tect an alter ego that works like a magic trick, letting her live
more than one life at once.

Whatever you think of her, there's Sagittarius energy jan-
gling in practically everything Miley Cyrus does. Mostly she
embodies a particular brand of Sagittarian magical thinking
that holds that the universe is infinitely expansive, big enough
to hold even the biggest life you can dream for yourself; that
the universe is infinitely welcoming, infinitely yielding, and
that a costume change can be enough to transport you over
the edge of your own life's boundaries and onto another plane.
According to this way of thinking, a person might never have
to limit themself, never have to make an irrevocable choice.
A person's restlessness can be sated with endless, infinite motion and change.

This is something wholly different from a possessive drive
to "have it all" or reach a point of fixed success. For Sagittarius, the desire is shifting and undefined. This is a drive, above
all else, to see, to learn, to experience, to continually seek
knowledge. It's a drive to live a life that never asks or requires
that you cede your freedom and never requires you to stop
searching. The *Hannah Montana* theme song, "Best of Both
Worlds," offers a cheesy but accurate Sagittarian thesis statement: "Yeah, you get to be a small town girl / But big time
when you play your guitar," Cyrus sings. "The best part is that
you get to be whoever you wanna be . . . "

FIRST THERE WAS ONIKA TANYA Maraj, a Sagittarius, born December 1982. Onika Maraj became Nicki Maraj, and Nicki Maraj became Nicki Minaj. And from early on, Nicki Minaj wasn't *only* Nicki Minaj but always also somebody else: the girly, pink-clad Harajuku Barbie; or the angry, outspoken Roman Zolanski; or Roman's rule-conscious mother, Martha. Or Nicki Lewinsky or Nicki Minaj LLC or any number of other alternate selves.

Her rapid donning and shedding of personas has alternately irritated, puzzled, and dazzled reviewers, with some critics thrilling to the weird energy of all the different Nickis, and some wishing to see the "real" Nicki underneath the wigs and eyelashes. "What people don't know," Nicki told *Vibe*, in defense of her style, "is that before I was doing that craziness I was doing me . . . But once I started doing all that weird shit—I'm not mad at it, because it got everyone's attention, but I can sometimes forget that I come from a real authentic place in hip-hop." But then immediately she contradicts herself, offering a more interesting possibility—that the voices, the personas, the weirdness, don't stand in contrast to her "real" self, but rather are *part of* her real self. "Im not someone who got signed to a record label who said 'hey, maybe you should do weird voices.' No. This is all years of me learning me and my style . . ." Then she contradicts herself again—"But I always knew I wanted to come back to my original sound"—and still again—"and the album is going to be a plethora of different sounds." She keeps trying to distance herself from her "craziness" but just can't manage to fully disavow it. She loves the craziness, and she loves her original sound, too, and she loves "all that weird shit." The best part, maybe, is that she gets to be whoever she wants to be.

FIRST THERE WAS JANELLE MONÁE Robinson, a Sagittarius, born December 1985. Then Janelle Monáe Robinson grew up to be just Janelle Monáe; then in 2003, when Monáe was eighteen and self-released her demo album *The Audition*, she became something else, something more than, something alongside her real human self. After three tracks about life and love and clubbing in Atlanta ("Jump in the shower. / Grab my towel and put my V. secrets on . . . And brush my teeth cuz I'm almost ready to roll," she sings in "Party Girl"), the fourth track, "Metropolis," opens a door to another universe altogether. Suddenly, here, she's singing as Cindi Mayweather, a cyborg worker in the fictional city of Metropolis, where an underclass of sentient, feeling cyborgs is enslaved by the human population. Cindi has broken the rules by falling in love with a human man, and over the course of this demo—and continued on Monáe's next three projects—she escapes from Metropolis, eludes bounty hunters and police, and eventually returns, now a messianic figure, to save her people, the androids of Metropolis.

Musically speaking, it's a wildly ambitious album, the songs skipping and jumping and sliding across and between genres, R&B to punk to soul to psychedelic. Reviewers spoke rapturously of Monáe's energy, musicianship, and range of genres and abilities; in both its vision and its execution, the project was dazzling, flashy, big. But in the long-running relationship between Janelle Monáe and Cindi Mayweather, there's something more intimate. Monáe appears on her album covers *as* Cindi—an image of her head atop a silvery robot, bar codes on her skin. Cindi feels less like a character that Monáe is playing, or a costume that can be easily put on and taken off again, than a vital part of Monáe. Janelle animates Cindi and brings her to life, but there's a sense of reciprocity here, a sense that Cindi brings Janelle to life as well. She offers her the space and freedom to go artistically wild, to do whatever she wants to do.

TRADITIONALLY, SAGITTARIUS IS THE ARCHER—not a human archer, but a centaur, half human and half horse. It's the first of the zodiac signs to be represented by a mythological creature; this mythic energy instills in Sagittarius a spirit of hybridity, of magical possibility, of a world in which even the impossible might, with some luck, become real. And this mythic hybrid energy overlaps perfectly with another kind of weird hybridity: the performer and their alter ego. Part middle schooler and part pop star, or part rapper and part Barbie doll, or part human and part cyborg savior. This is one way to wrest abundance from a stingy world.

The restless Sagittarian desire for expansiveness and freedom can be traced to the fact that Sagittarius is a fire sign—active, creative—and also a mutable sign. Mutable signs come at the end of a season, marking the transition from one to the next—from fall to winter, in this case. They're the signs most able to adapt, and they're the signs that thrive most on change. The combination of the bold fire element with the mutable quality of adaptation means that Sagittarius is likely to actively seek out change, to follow it, to make it happen.

This is a fundamentally optimistic energy; to willingly seek out change requires a certain amount of optimism that the world still holds enough good in it to make the risk of change worth taking. It requires an optimism that change is at least as likely to bring new joy as it is to bring new worry or failure or grief.

This optimism comes, in part, from Sagittarius's ruling planet of Jupiter—the planet of higher purpose, of abundance and generosity, of luck and possibility. Jupiter can teach us to expand our desires; more than that, it can make us brave enough to *want* to expand our desires by allowing us to believe that these big, bright wants might someday be satisfied. Jupiter can make us believe in ourselves; it can make us believe in anything. Under Jupiter's influence, Sagittarius encourages us all to believe that it's possible to expand the boundaries of what is knowable, to expand the limits of ourselves and of the very universe.

This can be seen as both a direct reaction to, and a marked break with, Scorpio's energy of intensity, secrecy, and privacy. If Scorpio's guiding principle is that one must be vigilant of the world's secret, underlying darkness, Sagittarius's guiding principle is that one must be open to undiscovered higher truths above our heads. If Scorpio is focused on probing the depths, Sagittarius is about looking up and out, to the mountains, to the skies, to the heavens. If Scorpio is focused on uncovering the hidden truth, Sagittarius is about exploration, about seeking out the world's abundant multiple truths.

Similarly, while both Scorpio and Sagittarius can be rebellious signs, their defiance comes from different impulses, and manifests in different ways. Scorpio is more likely to find a thrill, an electric charge, in the act of rebellion, or provocation, or boundary crossing itself. Sagittarius's rebellious energy is less pointed than this. For Sagittarius, disobedience is more often a necessary means to an end. There's no thrill in the provocation itself, only in the freedom that can be found on the other side. In a perfect world, Sagittarius would likely find it preferable for the borders to simply be dissolved altogether— for them never to have existed at all, not even for the sake of being broken.

SAGITTARIUS'S DESIRE FOR EXPANSION AND exploration can show itself in quite literal ways. Most introductory astrology books will tell you that Sagittarius is the sign of travel, particularly over long distances, across oceans, internationally. But in an age of easy luxury travel, it's important to clarify that it isn't the resort vacation or the Instagrammable trip to Reykjavik or Mexico City that's most emblematic of Sagittarian energy. For Sagittarius, the point isn't any of the tangible rewards travel can bring. The point is the movement itself. The point is in the way it's possible to feel so much at home while so far from home, so much at home while in motion.

This energy of questing and searching and journeying doesn't only manifest in physical ways. It can be intellectual; it can be metaphorical. It can make Sagittarius appear restless and unreliable; to a person focused on achieving a specific result, Sagittarius's looser focus on general movement and change can be maddening. Conversely, though, Sagittarius energy can feel freeing; it can give us permission to explore the world beyond the spaces we think we're allowed, beyond our natural range. Even when it's unfocused, restlessness can be empowering. For Sagittarius, huge changes— breaking up, quitting jobs, moving across the country—can feel more invigorating than scary, even when they've been poorly thought out, and even when they turn out to have been the wrong move. Sagittarius's highest purpose is to seek knowledge, but in everyday life, its actions often appear less lofty than that. If Sagittarius can't travel the entire world, they might delight in listening to strangers tell their stories. If they can't know everything, they might still try to read everything they possibly can. If they can't change their entire lives, they can still change their jobs, or their hair, or their mind. Even in limiting circumstances, even in a mundane life with no opportunity to build multiple lives using wigs like Miley or voices like Nicki, Sagittarius can reach for freedom in smaller ways.

AFTER ALL, AN ALTER EGO doesn't have to be as literal as a Hannah Montana or a Nicki Lewinsky. Through fluid, restless movement between genres—here funk, now hip-hop, now indie pop—Janelle Monáe has constructed a similar creative space for herself. And, for the most part, critics and fans have decided that this stylistic restlessness worked, that Monáe's sheer vocal talent and the front-to-back high quality of the music prevent any sense of incoherence or disjointedness.

But where the general critical consensus seems to be that Monáe's expansive vision coheres in the end into a stunning and exceptional product, the restless Sagittarius optimism can just as easily cross the line into sloppiness. It's not uncommon for Sagittarius energy to find itself altogether too unfocused to easily undertake the long, slow, earthly work of developing true mastery in a subject.

Not everyone is willing to overlook messiness for the sake of energy and forward motion, and messiness doesn't always produce worthwhile results anyway. In her post–Disney Channel career, Miley Cyrus has careened haphazardly through styles and sounds and identities, seemingly without any solid ground beneath her, without a purpose other than to break free from the squeaky-clean prison of her Disney image. And just as the very word "exploration" is linked to histories of colonialism— seeking out other places and cultures not to learn but to plunder—Miley Cyrus has come under continual fire for shallowly appropriating sounds, looks, and styles from hip-hop culture (wearing gold grills, for instance, or twerking onstage at the 2013 MTV Video Music Awards, or wearing dreadlocks to the 2015 VMAs), then pivoting away again in the face of criticism.

Reviews of her albums typically observe a mood of messiness or disorder or convolutedness. Sometimes this is followed with a qualifier—messy *but* honest, or all over the place *but* with some great pop anthems—sometimes not. In a review of Cyrus's 2019 EP "She Is Coming," *Rolling Stone* said, not entirely kindly, that "she'll never stop experimenting with other people's sounds. She *can't* stop."

Although Sagittarius isn't typically a sign that thrives on drama, this kind of loose and free approach to the world can sometimes lead there anyway. Its willingness to speak bluntly and openly can lead to all kinds of trouble. In the lead-up to the 2015 VMAs—the same VMAs that Miley Cyrus hosted in dreadlocks—Nicki Minaj tweeted a complaint that if she were skinnier, if she were white, her video "Anaconda" might have been nominated for Video of the Year (rather than just Best Hip-Hop Video). Taylor Swift, *also* a Sagittarius, bluntly and inadvisably tweeted that Minaj was "pitting women against each other." Miley Cyrus then told the *New York Times*—"In between freshly rolled joints," as the *Times* noted—that she didn't respect Minaj's statement because it was too angry. "Nicki Minaj," she said, "is not too kind."

Miley's tactless line illustrates the Sagittarian bluntness that inadvertently hurts feelings and starts trouble without necessarily setting out to do so. And after accepting her VMA for Best Hip-Hop Video, Nicki Minaj famously answered with some Sagittarian bluntness of her own. "Back to this bitch," she said—neither her voice nor her face giving even the slightest sign that she might be joking—"who had a lot to say about me the other day in the press: Miley, what's good." Some signs will internalize rudeness and harm, will bear lifelong grudges and make plans of slow-burning revenge. Sagittarius, instead, will directly and immediately strike back.

MILEY CYRUS'S POST–*HANNAH MONTANA* alter egos—the grills, the twerking, the stoner weirdness—may have sent her hurtling off the rails of pop respectability, but, if nothing else, they seem to have offered her a way out of an airless, constricting life of purity rings and bland, Disney-approved sweetness. The alter ego can be an active means for exploration and for expression, but it can function as a release valve, too. It can offer a way to break free from a box the world keeps trying to keep you in.

Britney Spears shows us what it can look like when a Sagittarius isn't allowed any restlessness at all, isn't given the chance to break free—although for a while, in her heyday, it almost looked like she did have an alter ego going, shifting constantly back and forth between the image of the innocent adolescent virgin and the sexually mature adult woman. Innocent but "not *that* innocent." "Not a girl, not yet a woman." And for a while back then the seeming contradiction worked for her. As Alice Bolin writes in *Dead Girls: Essays on Surviving an American Obsession*, much of her appeal rested on this winking dissonance. She gave the impression that she was aware of the effect she had and was playing along with it. But all these forces in her life—the pop music industry; her management; her audience's shapeless, hungry desire—wouldn't have given her a chance to *stop* playing along even if she'd wanted to. What looked on the surface like expansiveness was in reality a trap for her.

So in February 2007—after shifting away from her good-girl image, after two divorces, after countless disempowering and frightening run-ins with the paparazzi and the press, and immediately after one day in an Antigua drug rehab facility—she walked into a California hair salon and shaved her own head. At the salon, she said she was "tired of everybody touching me." When a photographer asked why she did it, she said, "Because of you." Hemmed in on all sides by surveillance and expectation and scrutiny and desire, she took what steps she could to be, or at least feel, free.

"The Tragedy of Britney Spears"—as *Rolling Stone*'s 2008 cover story titled it—is less about anyone's astrological makeup, of course, than it is about Spears being subjected to years of pressures and attentions that would be unbearable for nearly any of us. It's about fame and misogyny. Still, it's an instructive case for what happens when someone who needs freedom isn't given any at all, when someone who needs room to move and breathe and explore is watched and hounded every moment of the day, when someone who might like to grow and change and evolve is never given the chance. Sagittarius is, after all, a fire sign. Sagittarius will shave off their own hair if that's the only available path to independence.

Seven years earlier, Arundhati Roy, the author of *The God of Small Things* and a Sagittarius, had done something similar, cutting her hair off when the press's obsession with her feminine beauty became too heavy to carry; she refused to be known as "some pretty lady who wrote a book." She stopped writing fiction for twenty years. Sagittarius, after all, is a mutable sign and unafraid of change, unafraid of endings, unafraid to cut itself free, if need be. Roy chose to write political nonfiction and focus on activism during those twenty years.

And then she changed her mind again and in 2017 published another novel anyway.

I ENCOUNTERED JANELLE MONÁE'S MUSIC for the first time at my first post-college job, commuting every day from a dirty apartment in Brooklyn to a cubicle in Weehawken, New Jersey. The company that hired me sold, primarily via catalog, home goods and sexy men's underwear, and I spent my days in a haze of quiet tedium, taking sample photos of possible bedding arrangements for catalog spreads and writing bland product copy (which I was encouraged to steal, abundantly and without shame, from other catalogs), or fruitlessly trying, under the senior bedding merchandiser's tutelage, to learn to identify thread count by touch. Mostly, I spent my days producing spreadsheets of sales data on sheet sets and down comforters using information pulled from the company's clunky and unforgiving database.

Unlike any of the customer-facing jobs I'd had before this one, there was no demand that I perform busyness when I wasn't busy. The job itself was deeply, objectively boring, but it laid no claim to my feelings, to my interests, to the workings of my brain beyond those spreadsheets, and so I was free to dream and think and desire, to read long articles and chat with my friends online, and to plug my headphones into the computer and listen to Janelle Monáe's newly released *The ArchAndroid* over and over and over again.

It's hard for me now to access the feeling of absolute daz-
zlement I got when I listened to *The ArchAndroid* the first time,
the tenth time, the fortieth. The scope of the album's narrative vision, the range of its influences, the fluid slide from one
genre to the next—I understood that the world was bigger
than I had understood before now, and that more things were
allowed than I had been led to believe. The whole world, down
to my boring cubicle, hummed with potential. Right now I was
bored and broke, but every experience, even this one, surely
counted for something. Janelle Monáe had made herself a cyborg, and I wouldn't be stuck in this place forever. This might
sound outrageously, implausibly optimistic, but optimism is a
Sagittarius trait, and I believed in the unknown of the world
opening up to me.

Foolishly, though, I also scrolled through the YouTube com-
ments and saw one that brought me up short. Janelle Monáe's
whole *thing*, this person claimed—the weirdness, the android
alter ego, the black-and-white tuxedo uniform—was fake,
and they knew this because she hadn't always looked like
that, or sounded like that, or acted like that. She *used* to perform in denim miniskirts. I'm reconstructing this comment
from memory, lost as it is to the sands of internet time, but
my memory of it is vivid because it hurt my own Sagittarian
feelings. I thought that I was finally truly independent, able to
grow and change my mind and be whoever I wanted, but here
was a reminder of just how threatening change and freedom
can seem to some people. Change yourself at all, assert any

kind of freedom, and some dweeb will be watching and will swoop down to rat you out online. It made me wonder if I was actually a wishy-washy kind of person, a flake, unsure of who I really was. It made me wonder if the freedom that I wanted was simply *too much*.

An understanding of the sign of Sagittarius can offer us a way out of this kind of defeatist thinking. Its fiery energy can give us the strength to lean into optimism or boldness or weird and unclassifiable creativity. Its expansive view of the world can remind us of the value of taking chances, and trying out different lives. It tells us that an attempt, even a failed one, is as real as anything else, and that an alter ego can be as real as a "true" self. Cindi Mayweather let Janelle Monáe tell a kind of truth. Roman Zolanski let Nicki Minaj make noise she couldn't otherwise have made. Shaving her head turned Britney Spears from America's baby doll into America's tragic nightmare, and that, messy as it was, was an attempt at freedom, too.

I slowly began to embrace the Sagittarian fire in me. I quit my job and got a new one, and then I quit that job and got a new one, and then I quit that job, too. I left New York to move to New Orleans, then I left New Orleans to move back to New York, then I left New York again. And rather than making me feel destabilized or depleted, all this change made me feel powerful, alive, and happy to be in motion. It wasn't only my physical self that was in motion, either. Along the way, I started to get into astrology, and it offered me a whole new set of tools for seeking truth; it opened the door to a beautiful, utterly unexpected world of knowledge. Writing horoscopes gave me a way to break free from the unsatisfying work I did during the day, and free from the rigid intellectual structures that had followed me all through school. I didn't even see it at first, but astrology offered me a Sagittarian alter ego as well. First there was Claire Comstock-Gay, a Sagittarius born November 1987, then there was Madame Clairevoyant.

CAPRICORN

The Intellectual

A LONG TIME AGO, AT A VERY LOUD PARTY IN A PROBABLY HAUNTED HOUSE IN NEW ORLEANS, WHILE MUSIC THUMPED IN THE LIVING ROOM, I SAT ON THE BACK PORCH STEPS TALKING TO A WOMAN ABOUT ASTROLOGY. She was a Capricorn and wanted to know what I could tell her about her sign: she wanted to know what I could tell her about herself.

When I told her that Capricorn is typically understood to be the sign of discipline and boundaries, worldly success and growing up, she looked theatrically behind us into the house: where the empty beer cans overflowed from the kitchen trash can, where all the furniture smelled like wet dogs, where a bad romance was currently, dramatically coming to an end. This was a house where food scraps were being dropped and abandoned so chaotically through the house that the next morning my roommate and I would find pretzel crumbs ground not just into the floors and couches but the windowsills, the inside of the refrigerator, the grout between the bathroom tiles.

If I'm supposed to be so grown-up, this woman's face said, *then tell me what I'm doing here?* Two possible meanings, two possible feelings, lay coiled up inside that expression. The first possibility was that she saw some truth in that description of her sign and was expressing an ironic dismay over the distance between the maturity of her soul and the juvenile and self-indulgent squalor she found herself currently in. The second possibility was the reverse: that she was enjoying herself at this party full of happily immature people and was expressing an ironic dismay that the description of her sign could be so clueless about the reality of her life. Maybe the true feeling was something in between, a complicated blend of both.

In my experience, ambivalence is not an uncommon reaction when solar Capricorns learn about their sign. In popular astrology, Capricorn can be misunderstood so deeply that people with that sun sign turn away from astrology altogether. It isn't, of course, the only sign to be painted in reductive terms: Gemini has an unfair reputation for "craziness," and Scorpio has an unfair reputation for darkness so intense it verges on evil, but at least these two are misunderstood in ways that can seem fun or sexy or exciting. At least Gemini's alleged villainy offers some thrills; at least Scorpio's offers some glamour. Misunderstandings and oversimplifications about Capricorn, however, run along much more boring lines. Capricorn is depicted as the businessperson, the striving middle manager, the high school vice principal drunk on his own authority. Capricorn is described as though it has no claim to joy or romance, no capacity for imagination.

For example, here is the opener of the Capricorn section of *Astrology Understood,* a guidebook from 1946: "Endowed with an aspiring, determined, serious mind, with much reserve and self-control, [Capricorn] is greatly interested in the acquisition of a business of his own." In Linda Goodman's enduring classic, *Sun Signs* (1968), she advises that the best place to look for a Capricorn is in a group of people in "the upper income level. You can also try the middle income level, but the lower you go beneath that, the smaller your chances of finding a Capricorn." And here's Susan Miller introducing Capricorn in *Planets and Possibilities: Explore the Worlds Beyond Your Sun Sign* (2001): "Capricorn has a dream, and it is all about power and success. In your fantasy you can see your name engraved on a plaque on your door, the sterling silver case that holds your business cards, and the view of the glittering city that serves as a backdrop to your corner office."

Astrology has evolved and changed even since 2001, but this kind of thinking still informs our ideas today, even though, in my experience, it simply doesn't ring true. The Capricorns I've loved have been college dropouts and freelancers, adjuncts and food service workers. And the Capricorns I've loved have been the ones to tell me most often that they just can't find a way to identify with their Capricorn sun; they can't find a way to cut through all the noise.

Maybe, if the world's opportunities had been more equitably distributed, most Capricorns *would* in fact have been interested in the acquisition of a business of their own; maybe they *would* have ended up in the upper-income level. On the other hand, astrology existed before business as we know it existed at all, before the stock exchange or the industrial revolution, before anyone ever put on a suit and tie. While the figure of the businessperson might be one possible expression of Capricorn's energy, it isn't a foundational category of person at all. Astrology is old enough that Capricorn once meant something different, and that means it can mean something different again. What else could Capricorn look like if we could only learn to see it? If we broke Capricorn down to its basic parts, how could we reassemble them into another shape?

SO LET'S RETURN TO THE very basic building blocks of Capricorn: the symbol, the element, its quality, and its ruling planet.

Capricorn's constellation is the goat. Traditionally, it has been associated with the mythic "sea goat"—a creature with the head and body of a goat, and the tail of a fish—but in the contemporary iconography it's most often depicted as a mountain goat scaling a craggy peak.

Like its cousins Taurus and Virgo, Capricorn is an earth sign, and this earth sign energy is most alive not in dreams or emotions or the abstract workings of the mind but in the realm of physical, material reality. This can mean caring about one's physical surroundings: an earth sign is most likely to care about choosing the right color to paint the walls, and least likely to be satisfied living in a dirty apartment cluttered with other people's things. This isn't about fussiness, necessarily; it's more the sign of a person who notices the physical world very deeply, who lives on the material plane full-time.

And for this cardinal sign—the signs that mark the start of a season and that embody an energy of initiative and forward motion—its earth sign energy focuses not *only* on the realities of the here and now but also on moving toward a concrete, material future. This is the sign most comfortable working toward long-term goals, most comfortable with advancement over time, most comfortable choosing a point on the horizon and moving toward it with an unwavering certainty.

But it's Capricorn's ruling planet of Saturn that imbues it with so much of its aura of authority and control. Saturn is the planet of discipline and limitations, of authority and rules, and its influence can be a fearsome and challenging one. If the moon bears the energy of the archetypal mother, nurturing and soft, Saturn is the opposite: the archetypal father, distant, demanding, and strict. Traditionally, Saturn is one of the so-called malefic planets. Along with Mars, these are the planets of problems and difficulties, even bad omens—the planets that traditionally marked points of trouble or warning in an astrological chart.

But difficulty isn't the same thing as evil; being challenged is far from the same thing as being cursed. In her 1976 classic, *Saturn: A New Look at an Old Devil*, Liz Greene helped to crucially rehabilitate Saturn's image and to deepen our understanding of what it can do. Saturn, she wrote, isn't only the planet that represents the pain of our limitations. Rather, Saturn also shows us how "an individual may utilize the experiences of pain, restriction, and discipline as a means for greater consciousness and fulfillment." Limitations, in other words, are necessary and natural and good. Discipline doesn't have to be something handed down by a hard-hearted cosmic father but can be a tool, too.

COMBINED, THESE THREE BASIC ELEMENTS—THE earthy focus on material reality, the cardinal ambition and drive, and Saturn's influence over discipline and authority— make Capricorn the sign most concerned with hard work and material success, most concerned with its status and place in the world. Where Sagittarius, directly before it in the zodiac, is content to wander, motivated by the joy of exploration it- self, that isn't enough for Capricorn. Capricorn is motivated by the dream of advancement and recognition; its energy is too focused, too serious, to bother doing something if there isn't a goal in mind. If Capricorn is going to try to do a thing at all, they're likely to try to do it *well*, to try to be the best and to be recognized as the best.

It makes perfect sense that this would be interpreted to mean that Capricorn is the sign of career goals, but there's space to interpret it more widely, too. It might be more ac- curate to think of Saturn as the planet that represents the work you choose to do in the world, whether or not that work relates to business, whether or not that work is for pay. Capri- corn isn't willing to labor for no reward at all, but that doesn't mean that the reward has to be money.

SUSAN SONTAG, A CAPRICORN SUN (her Mercury and Venus were in Capricorn, too), offers us a model of a classic Capricorn who nevertheless was, at least according to her son, "profoundly uninterested in money." He has written that he can't ever remember her using a financial metaphor in conversation except for once, in a 1975 interview in the *Boston Review*: "My life is my capital, the capital of my imagination." Here Sontag gives us the chance to envision Capricorn differently. If traditional descriptions of Capricorn have a heavy focus on money—the drive to accumulate it and desire to spend it well—we might instead replace this with life or imagination or intellectual capital.

Although Sagittarius, the centaur with a bow and arrow, the questing thinker, is more commonly understood to be the philosopher of the zodiac, Capricorn provides a vision of a different kind of thinker. Because there is a difference between simply having a philosophically oriented mind and doing the long-term, structured work of engaging with the world intellectually. There's a difference between simply asking big questions and methodically following through on those questions and a difference between intellectual curiosity alone and the discipline to turn one's curiosity into a structured, committed system of engaging with the world. Where Sagittarius sometimes lacks rigor, Capricorn has it in abundance. Where Sagittarius finds satisfaction in the journey itself, Capricorn can translate ideas into an excellent finished work. Capricorn can demonstrate an intellectual practice that engages with the material realities of the world. Capricorn can demonstrate a dedication to one's commitments and a willingness to follow through.

Sontag wasn't the only Capricorn to use that driving, striving energy to build ideas instead of wealth. Simone de Beauvoir, whom Sontag frequently cites in her diaries, did the same. What space might be created if we imagined Capricorn not as the sign of the CEO but of the thinker, the public intellectual?

SONTAG, CRITICALLY, WAS NOT JUST any writer: she was one who managed to climb to the top and to be recognized—not only respected within her field but broadly famous as a thinker. She was well-known and easily recognized by her face and that silver streak zinging through her dark hair, made famous by book covers and television appearances. She was notable enough to have been profiled by *People* in 1978; in the profile, she presented the very picture of a world-class, materially successful figure, wearing "Saint-Laurent black slacks, blue Irish knit turtleneck and black lizard Lucchese boots," and talking about such material pleasures as buying books constantly, going out for Japanese food, and dancing with her artist friends at Studio 54. (Rather mischievously, she also told *People* she was not currently dating "anybody particularly thrilling.")

Capricorn is, after all, an earth sign, associated not only with the sea goat and the mountain goat but also, sometimes, with the god Pan—half goat and half man, impudent and lusty and closely connected to the earth. Like all earth signs, Capricorn has an appreciation for the physical pleasures of existence.

Compared to Taurus, though, Capricorn is less lazily hedonistic; compared to Virgo, Capricorn is less focused on the joys of a healthy body and a well-ordered space. Capricorn, rather, tends to find satisfaction in quality and good taste, whatever that looks like to them, over lavish abundance: like Saint-Laurent slacks, for example, and a good pair of boots.

At the same time, Sontag's profile is clearly not a picture of somebody whose primary motivation in the world is the accumulation of money. Sontag described being kicked out of her building so that her landlord could move into the unit himself, and the indignities of New York City apartment hunting. People told her, she said, that she should hire somebody else to do this work for her, assuming her fame and status translate directly to wealth. Her income at this time, says the profile, fluctuated between $8,000 and $18,000—about $30,000 to $70,000 in 2019, placing her well beneath Linda Goodman's "upper income level." "I'm just a working writer," Sontag is quoted as saying.

That may be technically true, but calling herself "just" a working writer is understating the case somewhat. While prestige and achievement shouldn't be offered as a reasonable replacement for pay, they can, to some Capricorns, be as motivating, if not even more motivating, than the money. For Susan Sontag, her intense hard work did result in rewards and recognition—maybe not riches, not her name engraved on a plaque on a corner office door, but her name on the covers of stacks of books.

SONTAG'S AMBITION SHOWED UP EARLY in her life. By the time she was fifteen, she'd graduated from high school. By the time she was eighteen, she'd graduated from college. This precocity led to a prolific professional life: she would ultimately publish four novels, two short story collections, four plays, and ten books of nonfiction. Her style tended toward the densely scholarly; Janet Malcolm called her first novel "a very advanced kind of experiment in unreadability."

This high-minded erudition may have made Sontag's work less accessible, but it also points to the rigor and intellectual labor that went into it. Her work drew its strength not just from some wellspring of natural brilliance but on hard work and the ambition to be excellent. Her journals show a methodical, conscientious mind at work: the lists she kept of books she read and films she watched take up pages and pages; she listed words she liked and connections between ideas. It gives the impression of a mind constantly firing on all cylinders, an intellect constantly at work. "While we watch reruns of 'Law & Order,'" Janet Malcolm wryly observed in the *New Yorker* in 2019, "Sontag seemingly read every great book ever written." This is the Capricorn work ethic in action: constantly climbing, constantly committed to the work. Sontag herself joked about the intensity of her work ethic in a 1979 interview with *Rolling Stone*, saying that when she first smoked weed at the age of twenty-two, it "changed [her] nervous system." Prior to this, she continued, laughing, "I didn't know you were supposed to relax or that it was any good or anything would come of it."

"Miss Sontag drives herself hard, more often than not," noted a 1966 *New York Times* review of *Against Interpretation*, "in the interest of adequacy of response." And, indeed, Capricorn is a sign that drives itself hard, nearly all the time. But the phrase "adequacy of response," too—which sounds, in our era of ecstatic praise, so faint as to be practically insulting—is fitting praise for a Capricorn. It echoes Virginia Woolf's famous praise of *Middlemarch* by George Eliot, a Capricorn moon: "one of the few English novels written for grown-up people." Both sound, on the surface, to be almost laughably restrained, but a Capricorn is likely to find value in this restraint. Capricorn isn't a sign that is willing to accept overstated praise. It's a funny bind to be caught in: Capricorn deeply needs recognition for their work but can't accept recognition that they don't feel is deserved. It's a kind of inner conflict that can lead to melancholy, even self-loathing.

In 1978, Susan Sontag published an essay in the *New York Review of Books* about Walter Benjamin called "Under the Sign of Saturn." In it she discussed Benjamin's resistance to modern psychological labels, choosing instead to think of himself in the "traditional astrological sense" as "a melancholic," someone who "came into the world under the sign of Saturn."

I've tried but cannot find the "traditional astrological" sense in which Benjamin might astrologically be said to have been born under the sign of Saturn. (His sun was in Cancer.) As far as I can tell, Benjamin was born "under the sign of Saturn" in the loosely metaphorical sense of having a gloomy "satur-nine" disposition. Sontag, on the other hand, very clearly *was* born under Saturn's specific astrological influence. While she made no such connection in the essay, it's difficult to read her thoughts about Saturn's influence on Benjamin without wondering whether she might, even if unconsciously, be writing about the Saturnian Capricorn energy animating her, too.

"The mark of the Saturnine temperament is the self-conscious and unforgiving relation to the self . . . ," she wrote of Benjamin. Further developing the theme of the Capricorn as someone who is self-critical to the point of being self-loathing, she writes that the Saturnine personality is likely to blame "its undertow of inwardness" on an insufficiently strong will. They're likely, then, to overcorrect, making such excessive efforts to strengthen their will that they become "compulsively" devoted to work.

Sontag could hardly have come up with a more accurate descriptor of Capricorn if she tried. For Capricorn does, often, feel a compulsive devotion to work. Sometimes, as with Benjamin, devotion to work can lead Capricorn into an endless cycle of striving to prove their worth—even in areas that have nothing to do with work or worthiness. Capricorn can believe, sometimes, that it's necessary to work hard to earn *everything*—not just jobs and wages but love, friendships, basic kindness. It follows that Capricorn can find it strangely difficult to accept that love might ever be freely given, that happiness can arrive by chance.

Similarly, Capricorn can sometimes find it difficult to understand that love is a normal human need. At the beginning of *As Consciousness Is Harnessed to Flesh*—the volume of her journals covering 1964 to 1980—Susan Sontag is coming off of a breakup, and her writing gives the impression of a mind circling around and around the experience of this heartbreak, trying to make sense of it by examining the dynamics of her childhood, and by excavating her emotional state with clear and devastating prose. But she isn't—at least, not in these journals—ever able to relax into the simple truth that she's a human who has been hurt, a human with a human need for love, and that there's no way to "earn" another person's love, only to find it, lose it, feel it. "I valued professional competence + force," she wrote elsewhere, "thinking (since age four?) that that was, at least, more attainable than being lovable 'just as a person.'" This kind of self-denying rigor of thought can sometimes cause other people to feel judged by Capricorn. And this can feel surprising to the Capricorn, who is, more than likely, engaged in an entirely personal, inward-looking variety of judgment. "If I can't bring judgment against the world, I must bring it against myself," Sontag wrote in one of the journals later published in *As Consciousness Is Harnessed to Flesh*.

In personal relationships, Capricorn's disciplined emotional rigor can be a heavy burden. Publicly, however, Capricorn's discipline can lead to a strong sense of responsibility to the world. Devotion to the work, after all, is how Sontag managed to read and write all those books. It makes Capricorn reliable, not just as in an everyday, around-the-house kind of way, but as a thinker. Capricorn can think with precision and responsibility, and can show us how we might make ourselves useful to the world.

Under Saturn's influence, Capricorn is deeply serious about the commitments it makes—whether practical, emotional, or intellectual—and tries hard to live accordingly. As Simone de Beauvoir is quoted as saying in Sontag's journals: "To smile at opponents and friends alike is to abase one's commitments to the status of mere opinions . . ." This kind of commitment tends, in our world, to be a deeply undervalued quality. It's not flashy or exciting, and in its steadiness it doesn't lend itself easily to narrative or drama. But it's one of the best, most beautiful, most needed things about Capricorn: they have the will and the discipline to honor their commitments.

Sometimes, this can be as basic as following through on aesthetic commitments: in a 1979 interview with *Rolling Stone*, Sontag discussed her aversion to lyricism and images in her writing. "Somebody says . . . 'The road is straight as a string' . . . There's such a profound part of me that feels that 'The road is straight' is all you need to say and all you should say . . ."

But Capricorn's commitments are often much broader in scope. Even though it's often described as a sign that is essentially moderate in demeanor—unlikely to take particular pleasure in stirring the pot—that doesn't mean that it pulls its punches or is afraid to take a stand. Sontag, for example, has drawn considerable right-wing ire for writing that "American power is indecent in its scale," and that "America was founded on a genocide . . . ," and, most famously, that "the white race is the cancer of human history . . ." When Capricorn holds steadfast, even to radical political commitments, they won't be afraid to back those commitments up.

Honoring commitments doesn't, of course, preclude change. Susan Sontag's ideas and commitments changed over time. For example, she eventually regretted the comparison of the white race to cancer, considering it inappropriate to use illness as a metaphor for the violence humans do to one another. She also came to change her mind about communism, drawing the ire of her friends on the left this time for publicly speaking about European communism's recent record of repression and violence.

Capricorn's energy can show us how to honor our commitments—even when honoring them means coming under the attack of political enemies, and even when it means coming under the attack of political *friends*. Even as those commitments evolve and change, and even as they require *us* to change. It can also show us that honoring our commitments doesn't have to translate to a life of conservative stodginess. Take, for instance, Capricorn Simone de Beauvoir's famously complicated and much-discussed decades-long relationship with Jean-Paul Sartre. They didn't live together or marry; both carried on simultaneous romantic and sexual relationships with other people. The agreement was that they remain intellectually committed to one another and that they tell each other everything. For more than fifty years, they did, and for all its unconventionality, this commitment has no less Capricorn energy than any other.

IN THE END, WE CAN learn so much more from Capricorn than simply how to slot ourselves into the world's existing power structures. The Capricorn businessperson is only one example of what this energy can do; an intellectual's commitment to knowledge can be just as Capricornian as a businessperson's commitment to money. Capricorn can show us how to choose our own commitments—intellectual, emotional, political—and stick by them. And Capricorn can show us, too, how the limitations and discipline we choose to adhere to don't make us weak; they make us strong. They provide the structure to let us rise through the world. They can make us powerful—without requiring us to give up our weirdness, or to oppress other people, simply through the force of our own steady discipline.

AQUARIUS

The Weirdo

IN 2003 THE MOVIE *MONA LISA SMILE* WAS RELEASED. It starred Julia Roberts as a free-spirited art professor at Wellesley College in 1953, doing battle with regressive ideologies, small-minded colleagues, and her young female students' internalized sense that the world had nothing more to offer them than marriage and domesticity. Her job, as she sees it, is to make it possible for these girls to break the rules they had previously considered unbreakable: to consider a life beyond the edges of the world they know, to consider what possibilities might lie past the sedate social safety of the wealthy, white world they inhabit. It is, by and large, an unremarkable story—standard fare for a Hollywood movie looking back to the fifties—with the exception of one memorable scene that gets stolen completely by an off-screen Aquarius.

In this scene, Julia Roberts—ever the bohemian with her hair worn loose, dressed in black clothes and a beret—brings her tweed-suited students, their hair set in stiff, glistening waves, to an art gallery. A small crew of art handlers bustle around them, and the gallery owner tells Julia that they've arrived at the perfect time. Two of the workers pry open a large wooden crate, and its front crashes sonorously to the ground to reveal the contents. "There it is," says the owner. His voice is reverent. Roberts's face is rapturous. Violins start to play.

Inside is a painting: *Number One, 1950 (Lavender Mist)* by Jackson Pollock, an Aquarius. Black and gray and blue and orange paints are dripped and spattered across the mural-size canvas. The students look disturbed. Julia Roberts looks like a woman in love. She walks to the painting and stands close, her black-clad figure standing in elegant contrast to the painting, which takes up the entire frame. Then the camera cuts in close, showing us the details of Pollock's brushstrokes, the layers of paint, the colors and lines. This painting, the camera tells us, is something potent, something new, something with the potential to change everything.

"I was just getting used to the idea of dead, maggoty meat being art," quips an unimpressed Ginnifer Goodwin, to giggles from her classmates. "Now *this*?"

"Do me a favor—do yourselves a favor," says Roberts. "Stop talking and *look*." She assures them that it's fine if they don't like the painting and that she won't assign a paper on it. Their only assignment is to "consider" it. When they've finished looking at this surprising, rule-breaking painting, they can go home. She leaves the students to carefully examine the painting—serious, wondering, considering.

These rich teenagers, the movie implies, have never seen anything like this—have never engaged with art so forward-thinking and modern and weird. All signs—their upturned faces, the plaintive violins, the camera's gentle roving close-ups over Pollock's densely layered colors—indicate that something is cracking open in these straight-laced young women. In the deepest corners of their minds, possibilities are beginning to stir and awaken. And while the Julia Roberts character brought them here, it's Jackson Pollock—an Aquarius—who is able, with the unexpected weirdness of his art, to reach through time and space and blow these teenagers' minds.

In spite of its gentle cheesiness, this scene is a near-perfect representation of Aquarian values. While there are different ways for a piece of art to act on its viewers—art can demonstrate technical mastery, or create beauty, or activate feeling, or serve as a mirror that reflects the existing world back to us—for Aquarius, art in its highest form is about breaking the rules, about transcending the everyday in order to experience the world anew. For Aquarius, the best kind of art can function as a time machine into a future we could never have imagined until the art showed us the way. It can create possibilities where none existed before. This is a sense of possibility that Aquarius can share with the rest of us. Aquarius can teach the rest of us how to dream, how to imagine, how to feel this electric feeling.

AQUARIUS IS REPRESENTED BY THE constellation of the Water Bearer: a person—usually a man or a boy—pouring water from a vessel. As a symbol it's evocative, but less straightforward and intuitively accessible than others in the zodiac— fitting, perhaps, that Aquarius's symbol requires a little more imagination. Where other symbols are based on what they *are*—a ram, a crab—the Aquarian symbol is based on an action: bringing water. The water it brings can be seen as imagination, or curiosity, or a willingness to break the rules. Aquarius understands how much we need all these things in order for our lives to really be livable; it understands that all these things are as necessary to life as water itself.

Aquarius offers us the feeling that every seemingly ironclad rule in the world is, in fact, breakable. Aquarius can offer the certain knowledge that every person or institution in a position of total power can still be defied; every idea that seems unassailable can still be questioned. Aquarius invites us to know what it knows: that you can get past all the people constantly pressuring you to be normal and conventional and unsurprising, and once you can get to the other side of all the world's rules and restrictions, there are whole galaxies of thought and creativity available to you.

More than any other sign, Aquarius values independence and freedom. More than any other sign, Aquarius can see the rewards that nonconformity can offer. Aquarius is willing to rebel and refuse, to turn away from what is accepted and normal. Aquarius is willing to seem strange, willing to be misunderstood—willing, if necessary, to go it alone.

Aquarius is also one of the more brainy, intellectual signs of the zodiac. In spite of the deceptive "aqua" in its name, Aquarius is not a water sign but an air sign, oriented toward thought and the intellect and the social, thinking world. Air signs, more than the signs of any other element, live in the head, and Aquarian energy is experienced largely in the brain. The most emblematic Aquarian art isn't the sweaty, throbbing, up-close physicality of a punk show, nor is it the emotionality of a movie with an ending so sad that audiences cry too hard to even see. It isn't designed to set a viewer's heart beating so much as to set their thoughts sparking. It's designed to activate not the body but the mind.

However, that isn't to say that Aquarius's braininess is a joyless landscape of straight lines and cold logic. It doesn't exist as some kind of sterile, restrictive foil to the lush world of the heart. Enduring Enlightenment values would have us believe that the intellect is tamer, more civilized, more respectable than the messy human body, but Aquarius can show us how wrong that really is: how intensely rangy and colorful and wild the mind can be. There's space here for imagination, for rule breaking, for endless weird surprises.

Aquarius's braininess also doesn't mean that its art is more analytical than art created from feeling. Gertrude Stein, an Aquarius, wrote *Tender Buttons* in 1914, a short book of modernist poetry that uses language to make the ordinary world wild and unknowable. "The change of color is likely and a difference a very little difference is prepared. Sugar is not a vegetable," says one poem in the collection. "PEELED PENCIL, CHOKE" is the title of another, followed by the single line "Rub her coke": clearly sexual, weirdly sexy, yet offering nothing that makes any sense according to the rules of everyday English. These poems feel like messages from a dimension close to but not quite touching ours. They feel like transmissions back in time from a human civilization a thousand years in the future, or from a parallel human society that branched off from ours a thousand years ago and developed, parallel to us, on the moon.

I encountered Gertrude Stein in college, in an American literature class where I felt too unprepared, too intimidated, too far intellectually surpassed by my classmates to raise my hand even one single time. "Great literature," our professor frequently said, "always evades any totalizing attempts at interpretation." Based on our class discussions, however, it hardly felt that way. Whether or not we were correct, we were all *constantly* putting forth totalizing attempts at interpretation. Until we reached Gertrude Stein, whose poems resist, almost magically, being analyzed. Like any other text, they *can* be the subject of analysis, of course, but they offer so little to really grab on to, so little that won't slip from your grasp when you try to hold on too tight.

And in this, they provided a feeling of total freedom from what I had previously understood to be the rules about making poems. They offered the sense that, all along, the possibilities have been broader than anyone was willing to say. All along, a poem could look like anything at all. Emily Dickinson, a Sagittarius, famously said that she recognized true poetry if she felt "physically as though the top of [her] head were taken off," but it turned out to be Gertrude Stein, an Aquarius, who really took off the top of my head, who alerted me to how wild and unconstrained a poem could be.

At the same time, this sharp and airy creative freedom can sometimes lead to Aquarius being accused of being detached—more focused on thought than on feeling, more interested in the ideas only they can see than in the people around them right now. For being one of the signs that value intimacy highly, Aquarius can be hard to get close to and hard to understand: Aquarius tends to feel less need for intimacy than many of the other signs. For Aquarius, relationships can be equally valuable at varying levels of closeness and distance; steady emotional intimacy isn't the only measure of care.

That's not to say that Aquarius is cold or unkind—it's still one of the likeable, social air signs. For all its weirdness, Aquarius can be fiercely and steadfastly kind. In famous Aquarius artist David Lynch's little book *Catching the Big Fish: Meditation, Consciousness, and Creativity*, he writes about how important it is to him *not* to direct his movies like a Hitchcock, like a Kubrick, like a dictator. The idea is not to coldly impose his ideas from on high but rather "to get everybody to come together and go down the same track—the track indicated by the ideas." Running the set like a dictator, he writes, would not only weaken the end product but also ruin the social pleasures of doing the work together: "There would be no fun in going down the road together. And it *should* be fun."

Not all rebellion has to be angry, after all; not all refusal must mean struggle and difficulty. It *should* be fun, as David Lynch writes, to imagine and create, to burst outside of existing structures, to flout the rules. Coming after Capricorn in the zodiac—and responding to Capricorn's intense respect for order, rules, and authority—Aquarius can remind us of the sheer joy of individuality and weirdness, the beautiful intensity of looking toward the future and believing in the possibility of change. Aquarius isn't just about rejection of the past, but about an active belief in the future. It's the sign of progress and discovery, technological advancement, and utopian thinking. It's the sign of David Lynch creating a non-profit foundation to teach children how to meditate. It's the sign of hippies and weirdos and dreamers: "No more false-hoods or derisions . . . let the sunshine in," goes the famous "Aquarius" song from *Hair*.

Beyond David Lynch's meditation practice, his artistic work, too—filled with aliens and dreams and travel between worlds—carries an Aquarian energy of transcending the ordinary to find something new. "I love going into another world," he writes in *Catching the Big Fish*, "and I love mysteries . . . I like the feeling of discovery."

Watching Lynch's work—particularly for the first time—can offer viewers a feeling of discovery of their own. *Twin Peaks*, for instance, is less formally strange than Lynch's movies but still much, much weirder than nearly anything else on television. While it has all the trappings of a top-notch detective show—a dead blond teenager, an unorthodox detective, a supporting cast alternating between wacky and sinister, a town full of secrets—what makes the show great is not in how it adheres to generic conventions but how it departs from them. Lynch's pacing tends toward the slow and the strange, and his narratives bend in unexpected shapes. Characters talk backward and walk between worlds, and owls are not what they seem, and even the police look for answers in the world of magic and dreams.

Years later, ABC would try to work with Lynch on another show, citing a desire to again produce something extraordinary and unlike the other shows on television. This one would be called *Mulholland Drive*—which would ultimately, after the network rejected the pilot, become Lynch's 2001 movie of the same name. The network's reason for rejecting the show seemed to be the same reason it wanted the show to begin with: it was too much unlike the other shows on television, and too much *like* David Lynch. "Their thinking process is very foreign to me," Lynch told the *New Yorker* about *Mulholland Drive*'s false start. "They like a fast pace and a linear story, but you want your creations to come out of you, and be distinctive. I feel it's possibly true that there are aliens on earth, and they work in television."

This story points to a classic Aquarius problem. True individuality can create absolute magic, but it can lead to underappreciation sometimes, too. People can *say* they value uniqueness, but, like the ABC executives, they lose their nerve once it really comes down to it. It can be so lonely for Aquarius to feel animated and inspired by the wildest questions and dreams and ideas, only to be met with people who seem to actually *like* the accepted way of doing things; people who seem to be made happy by routine and conformity; people who seem to have no desire at all for revolution and not even a desire for change. It can be so lonely to want *more* than the world holds now, to want to rebel and transcend, but not find anyone ready or willing to travel along with you.

People don't, after all, always *want* to have their minds blown. Sometimes it's because they're unimaginative or incurious, but just as often they're simply too busy fulfilling their physical needs to really sit down with Gertrude Stein's prickly poems; or they're too exhausted to put in the mental work to follow a wild and nonlinear TV show; or they're too busy organizing their workplace or falling in love to want to reach out to the very edge of the universe. Sometimes, people simply prefer more regular fare: paintings with identifiable images, detective shows that follow the rules of the genre. As much as Aquarius knows that this is a natural consequence of being ahead of one's time, other people's benign disinterest can still feel isolating. As much as Aquarius lives to be different from everyone else, that doesn't mean that it's easy, in the day-to-day, to be so far out in front of them. That doesn't mean it feels good to be misunderstood.

Toward the very top of the list of broadly misunderstood cultural figures, you'd likely find Yoko Ono, an Aquarius: most famous not for her art career but for "breaking up the Beatles." Her name remains shorthand for a bothersome girlfriend, a femme fatale, an intruder upon her male partner's valuable creative work—which is funny, because the lore has it that when she and John Lennon (a Libra sun and Aquarius moon) first met, at one of her art shows, they felt deeply understood by one another. For his part, Lennon felt understood by a piece in the show that required the viewer to climb up a ladder, at the top of which, they'd find the printed word YES. This wasn't, he concluded, artistic weirdness simply for the sake of creating a disturbance or embarrassing its viewers. Rather, it was artistic weirdness for the sake of some positive feeling: YES.

But, as Lennon told it, Ono wouldn't give him the time of day until he proved he could get on her level—get weird, too. He asked to participate in one of her pieces, which invited the viewer to hammer a nail into a painting. She told him he'd have to pay for each nail; he answered that he'd pay imaginary money if she gave him an imaginary nail. That, he said, was when they "really *met*."

In the retellings of this story more heavily marked by misogyny and racism, this was all calculated on her part: she recognized Lennon to be a wealthy superstar and wanted to steal some of his glow in order to aid her climb through the art world. In other retellings, though, including her own, she didn't recognize Lennon or know much about the Beatles at all. In these versions of the story, they recognized something true in each other, and the greater gift that passed between them wasn't Lennon's massive fame but her Aquarian weirdness. It offered him a way back into his own corresponding weirdness, into his own rebellion, and out of the limitations of the role he had become required to play.

Indeed, much of Ono's art can offer all of us a way back

into our own imaginations, our own weirdness. The conceptual pieces collected in her book *Grapefruit* read like instructions for accessing Aquarian energy. TOUCH POEM FOR GROUP OF PEOPLE, from 1963, instructs simply: "Touch each other." LAUGH PIECE instructs the performer to laugh for a whole week. EARTH PIECE instructs the performer to listen to the earth turning. A reader does not, obviously, need to literally follow these instructions: to do so, in many cases, would mean to break the laws of physics, or to transcend the limits of the human body. (One piece simply instructs the performer to fly.) Reading them is enough to start feeling the effects: new rooms suddenly open up in the mind; new images push the bounds of the imagination outward; new possibilities of relating to the world (*can* you listen to the earth turning?) begin to make themselves known.

I USED TO IMAGINE THAT the artists who could open the door to this feeling must have some kind of unique freedom, some special access to a different, purer, wilder kind of knowledge than the rest of us could ever find on our own. I thought that they possessed a special kind of superhuman genius that elevated them above the rest of us, a genius that freed them from the tyrannical constraints of everyday life and everyday thinking. And it's taken some work, some rethinking of the world and the people in it, to stop believing that genius is a special gift to the very few.

Much of the world, after all, has a vested interest in hiding our imaginations from us until we forget we ever had them at all. Much of the world has a vested interest in making rebellion seem always bleak, never bright. We're encouraged to misunderstand individuality and nonconformity in other people, or else to ignore and suppress it in ourselves, or to believe that we simply can't afford to think so big.

If these artists do have access to some special, secret quality, it might be related to Aquarius energy. And the beautiful thing about Aquarius energy is not that it's superhuman but that it's just *one way* of being human. Aquarius energy is a magic that touches all of us; it's a magic all of us can use. And we can look to the people who have harnessed it: the artists who opened doors, the artists who refused to be normal, the artists who believed in living their own way and weren't afraid.

I WAS A HIGH SCHOOL freshman before I learned that Yoko Ono was not just John Lennon's girlfriend, nor even just his musical collaborator, but an artist in her own right. I was at a museum, on a family trip to a nearby city, feeling desperate for independence, desperate to do something *different* to break out of the shell of everyday life that felt like it had hardened around me. I didn't want to be here and I didn't want to go home; I didn't want to be surrounded by all these people, and I didn't want to be alone, either. I wanted *out*, but out of what? And where to?

I wandered away from my family through the white-walled rooms of the museum, then came to a small television showing video of the sky. Not magnificent skyscapes: no sunrises or sunsets or storms, no framing mountains or city skylines, no special editing or effects. These were just the same regular, placid blue skies you might see if you simply went outside and looked up. As I would learn later, it was *precisely* the same regular blue sky I would have seen if I had gone outside and looked up: the piece was Yoko Ono's Sky TV, a twenty-four-hour live feed of the sky outside.

But I didn't know that yet, and I stood in front of the screen for a long time, looking for all the world like those teenagers in *Mona Lisa Smile*, considering the Jackson Pollock with confused sincerity. The feeling was that of a window opening. The feeling was of something strange and special revealing itself to me. Something that should not, based on my knowledge of the world, have been allowed was happening anyway: a tiny old television was showing me the blue sky, and a museum called it art. A rule I hadn't even been aware of had just been broken right in front of me, and my own world was better for it.

Later, I would tell my coolest, most Aquarian friend at school what I had seen at the museum. To my disappointment, she wasn't impressed. She already knew all about Yoko Ono. In fact, she told me, her favorite Ono piece was one called *Bottoms*. "She made all of these people walk on a treadmill and took close-up video of their hairy butts!" I didn't fully believe her—it sounded like exactly the type of thing a fourteen-year-old might make up—but she was right. And the electric feeling of possibility came over me once more, faced with this unbelievable evidence that, with enough courage and enough weirdness, a person could make any art she wanted and get away with it.

PISCES

The Guardian

I BEGAN WRITING THIS CHAPTER WHILE THE SUN WAS IN PISCES. It was a particularly brutal Pisces season in the city where I lived; a polar vortex brought a string of bitter days with wind chills down to -40°F, and once temperatures finally rose back into the single digits, the skies opened up and began dumping fresh snow over the city. The news had reported that an all-time record for snowfall was by now nearly inevitable, a possibility that held no real excitement or suspense. It was rare to leave the house without seeing a car stuck and spinning its tires in an icy intersection. My next-door neighbors gave up entirely, letting their car hibernate under several feet of snow until spring.

In the face of so much unrelenting cold, it felt nearly impossible to summon the drive to do much of anything. The only thing that felt easy—the only thing that came naturally at all—was *crying*. I cried to music by Nina Simone (a Pisces) and Chopin (a Pisces). I cried after reading a short story about loneliness, and after watching a video of an injured dog learning to walk again. I cried to the sound of my faraway friend's voice on the phone, telling me she missed me. I cried during arguments, and from feelings of despair and confusion, and from feeling loved, then unloved, then loved again. It sounds outrageous, and even at the time it felt that way, too—to be so overwhelmed by this bone-deep, uncontrollable emotion. I cried more while the sun was in Pisces than I did in all the previous eleven months of the year.

I SPEND SO MUCH OF my time as an astrologer trying to push back against the types of astrology that offer easy answers; against the limiting stereotype; against the easy shortcuts about the signs and their meanings. It's not that I mind astrology's proliferation in informal contexts like jokes and memes, although I know some astrologers find themselves driven to distraction by the flippant, rowdy, and frequently shallow—even incorrect—nature of astrology on the internet. And it's not that I begrudge anyone the value in condensing the signs' deep complexity into introductory, simplified versions: there's far too much there to be able to express all the nuance at once. Sometimes, though, we get so accustomed to the condensed version that we forget there's more. We get seduced by the comfortable pleasures in the easy ideas—like, for instance, the idea that Pisces is the sign of emotional overload and round-the-clock tears.

It's a reductive idea and one whose incessant repetition can make it more difficult to see Pisces clearly. But it's impossible to fully disavow, either, as it—like all the stereotypes of the signs—holds at least some truth.

Pisces is, after all, a water sign, and the water signs are united by their shared home in the fluid, mysterious world of emotions. The water signs recognize emotions as solid and important things—as real as our bodies, as valuable as our ideas, as powerful as the actions we take in the world. These are the signs that experience feelings most deeply, and that read the language of emotions most clearly, and that can most comfortably navigate the powerful undercurrents of feeling that flow through and around us all. These are the signs whose most vivid, intense experiences of life don't always happen on the surface, in the physical world. Water signs are interior and intuitive, with deep, dramatic, intense inner lives. For water signs, feelings aren't incidental, not afterthoughts, not secondary to anything else. Feelings are what the world is made of.

To people with placements concentrated in the other elements, this energy can be a little unnerving. It isn't always pleasant to know that somebody else is experiencing something deep and rich and invisible that you know nothing of. It can be maddening to watch somebody you love suffering from emotions that you can neither feel nor understand. It can even induce a kind of envy, knowing that someone is easily receiving messages transmitted on a frequency you can access only sometimes, haltingly, in quick flashes.

Although astrology offers us tools and frameworks for imagining and understanding other people's inner landscapes, it takes a tremendous amount of work and humility and time to try to actually understand the contours of another person's mysterious inner life. It can be much easier, instead, to focus on the external manifestations, the things visible in the physical world. For Pisces, as often as not, that external manifestation is crying, so when we look for Pisces's tears, it's easy enough to find them.

DURING MY LONG PISCES SEASON of tears, the thing that affected me most of anything was *Won't You Be My Neighbor?*, the 2018 documentary about Fred Rogers and his television show, *Mr. Rogers' Neighborhood*. The documentary treats Rogers's life mostly chronologically, and has hardly any real plot to speak of: neither the show nor Rogers's life seems to have offered much of the type of drama that makes for compelling narrative. (At one point, the movie asks people who knew Rogers well whether he was *really* as wholesome and kind as his public persona. They all answered yes.) Rather, what makes the movie compelling is the way it quietly unfurls Rogers's philosophy of love, showing that love in action in the world.

We see, for example, Rogers's deep, respectful kindness to a young boy in a wheelchair who is about to undergo major spinal surgery and who appears on the show to sing a song (the unbearably pure and tender "It's You I Like"—"I hope that you'll remember / Even when you're feeling blue / That it's you I like / It's you yourself / It's you."). We see Rogers kindly—and pointedly, during the civil rights movement— invite François Clemmons, who plays *Neighborhood*'s friendly local cop and who is Black, to soak his feet together with Rogers in a plastic kiddie pool. We see Yo-Yo Ma describe playing Bach on his cello to Rogers, over the phone, after finding out Rogers was dying of cancer.

As a non–water sign, I often wonder if I'm being manipulated when a movie that is *clearly* designed to make me cry does its job so well. But what else is there to do? We can work all our lives to harden our hearts against tragedy, to strengthen our defenses against cruelty . . . but to defend against real tenderness? Against real compassion and love for other people? Impossible.

And it was real compassion that flowed through the entire movie, undergirded by total, ego-less love from beginning to end. Over and over, in different ways, Fred Rogers reiterated his steadfast respect for the overwhelming power of our emotions and his commitment to do right by them. "Children have very deep feelings," he says in one clip, responding to the Bobby Kennedy assassination in 1968, "just the way parents do, just the way everybody does. And our striving to understand those feelings and to better respond to them is what I feel is the most important task in our world."

Fred Rogers, who believed so deeply in feelings, was a Pisces. And Rogers, who once testified to Congress that "if we in public television can only make it clear that feelings are mentionable and manageable, we will have done a great service," offers a way to understand Pisces in a slightly different fashion from that of the incessant weeper. Rogers offers a way to understand Pisces energy as something focused outward, toward other people, toward the world. In the movie, Rogers himself doesn't cry at all. Rather, he makes *us* cry. At its most powerful, Pisces can love the world in a way that makes feelings mentionable and manageable. Pisces understands how to live with and honor emotion—and how to show us to live with it, too.

TO UNDERSTAND PISCES, IT'S IMPORTANT to remember that it's the final zodiac sign of the year. This matters, because the signs build off each other and respond to each other on their path around the wheel of the zodiac. Pisces reacts to Aquarius's focus on ideas with a focus on feelings, and to Aquarius's vibe of cool intellectual distance with one of deep emotional intimacy. But still, Piscean intimacy maintains an awareness of the rest of the universe. Pisces's watery emotionality focuses on the depth of feeling that suffuses everything. It's about seeing that, as Rogers said, "love is at the root of everything. All learning, all parenting, all relationships. Love, or the lack of it." For Pisces, with its universal bent, it's crucial to pay attention not just to the feelings that live inside us individually but also to the ways that emotion, broadly speaking, is a vital component of our humanity, a force that is present and alive in everything we do.

Partly because of this broad, universal intuition, Pisces has a reputation for being the wisest, most spiritual sign of the zodiac. "Wisdom" is a word you'll hear constantly in discussions of Pisces. *Wisdom* specifically, which is not the same thing as *intellect* or *cleverness* or *smarts* (although they can exist together in the same person). There's a broader element of spirit, of connectedness to the world. Pisces is, after all, ruled by Neptune, the planet of dreams, intuition, and spiritual enlightenment. It gives Pisces a clear and intuitive view of the interconnectedness of all things; it lets Pisces viscerally feel the totality of the universe.

THIS DEEP, RICH, SPIRITUAL WISDOM can give Pisces a dreamy, artistic nature: the poet Hoa Nguyen once wrote that Pisces is the sign with the greatest number of astronauts and dancers. Pisces can also use this dreamy wisdom to create the best stories for children; Fred Rogers wasn't alone in this. Ezra Jack Keats, author of picture books like *A Letter to Amy*, *Peter's Chair*, and the Caldecott-winning *The Snowy Day* (1962), was a Pisces, too. Keats was white, the son of Polish-Jewish immigrants to New York City, but his were among the first mainstream children's books to feature children of color. *The Snowy Day*, his most famous work, simply follows a young boy, Peter, spending a day playing in the snow in New York. "None of the manuscripts I'd been illustrating featured any black kids—except for token blacks in the background," Keats is quoted as saying in Brian Alderson's *Ezra Jack Keats: Artist and Picture-Book Maker*. "My book would have him there simply because he should have been there all along."

Lois Lowry, author of young adult novel *The Giver*, is a Pisces, too. *The Giver* tells the story of a dystopian society in which all strife and conflict and pain, but also all emotion, have been replaced by a culture of total security and conformity called Sameness. Sameness also requires that all collective memory be withheld from the general population and kept by one person only: the Giver. The book's protagonist, a boy named Jonah, must work with the Giver to return feeling and memory to his people. When Jonah finally gains access to his emotions again, he sees in color for the first time in his life.

Louis Sachar, author of *Holes* and the *Sideways Stories from Wayside School* books, is a Pisces, too. The Wayside School books follow the adventures and escapades of a class of elementary school students on the thirtieth floor of a comically tall and occasionally supernatural school. The stories are funny and intimate, sometimes dark: in one, the strict Mrs. Gorf turns misbehaving students into apples; in another, Sammy the new kid turns out actually to be a rat dressed in many raincoats. And in another, a student tries unsuccessfully to sell her toes to the gym teacher for five cents each. While Rogers was steadfast in his insistence on an ethos of quiet gentleness and an absolute lack of scariness on his show, Sachar's warm and magical chaos is nurturing in its own way. For some kids to get temporarily turned into apples, and for some to unfairly get blamed for mischief, and for some to get teased by their friends, feels reflective of the world: a manageable and true amount of chaos, in exchange for a manageable and real amount of magic.

IT MIGHT SEEM OVERLY PRECIOUS, even anti-intellectual, to suggest that the deepest Pisces wisdom lends itself best to making art for children. But making art that children can connect to deeply is a rare and valuable skill requiring a rare and valuable kind of love. It isn't easy for adults to remember childhood as it really is: not a realm of sweetness and simplicity but of chaotic emotions and deep vulnerability. Fred

Rogers "never forgot how vulnerable it was to be a kid," said producer Margaret Whitmer in the documentary *Won't You Be My Neighbor?* "You know, you're this little thing. Everything else in the world is bigger than you are." It's a rare and valuable gift to create a story emotionally wise enough that children can feel respected, even in the middle of an emotional world as turbulent and wild and untamed as the sea.

Accessing the world of childhood emotions—for that matter, even accessing the world of adult emotions—is a power that's not always valued the way it should be. As much as contemporary wellness culture pays lip service to mental health and self-care, it's hard to see evidence that we live in a world that values feelings much. We're encouraged not to have darker, more difficult feelings at all, so we try to ignore them, or to explain them away, or to bargain our way out of having them in the first place. We try to wrap them up tight and hide them away where nobody else can ever see them, where even we can avoid touching them if we're careful. "Adulthood," according to much of the culture, comprises status markers like marriage and homeownership, a job and a 401(k). It's about economic productivity and a willingness to play by the rules.

For Pisces, however, adulthood likely means something altogether different: an ability to process feelings, to love and accept love, to value our deep connections to one another. For these Pisces creators, therefore, the purpose of creating stories for children isn't to prepare them to grow into productive *adults* (unlike the "Baby Mozart" CDs that claim to optimize brain development, or the Baby University books purporting, only partly tongue-in-cheek, to teach your toddler marketable skills like blockchain). Rather, the purpose is to tell stories that can prepare children to grow into *people*—people who are in touch with their inner lives, who have a sense of empathy for others, and who know themselves to be worthy of love. Wild feelings aren't meant to be grown out of but to be grown into. Love isn't an afterthought but the point.

To assert that feelings are so valuable can feel profoundly frightening to those who have been taught to suppress their own, to value their power or career or social status above all else. For no matter how soft Pisces seems, its gentle love can feel like a threat to anyone with a powerful enough ego. Pisces's insistence on emotion can feel like an implied rebuke to someone who has worked hard to avoid or outgrow their own softness. And, more often than not, when people imagine themselves to be threatened or reproached, they don't respond with kindness.

The more visible Mr. Rogers and his gentle, ego-less love became, the more his whole project was mocked and resisted. Eddie Murphy appeared in a series of *Saturday Night Live* parody skits as Mr. Rogers's gritty counterpart "Mr. Robinson," who used swear words, taught his audience how to sell stolen items on the street, and explained that Ronald Reagan's economic policies were the reason why he and his neighbors were poor. According to *Won't You Be My Neighbor?* Fred Rogers found this parody funny, even affectionate. Other attacks, however, were more straightforwardly mean: most notably, Fox News, along with other right-wing media, called him "an evil, evil man" for teaching children they were special and loved.

While Fox's vitriol is a sad and weird projection with no bearing on reality, astrological or otherwise, Pisces does have a so-called shadow side, just like the rest of the signs. This shadow is not nearly as dark as the "evil, evil" that Fox News imagined but runs closer to a vague directionlessness. Pisces might have broad, expansive ideas about the world but can still find it difficult to actually take action. It can be difficult to step outside of the deep and fluid world of feelings long enough to accomplish anything, to put in the work up here in the clear light of day. Pisces can be content, instead, just to feel.

Pisces can sometimes be self-pitying to the point of valorizing suffering. And this brings us back again to tears. This time, though, I want to think of them in a slightly different light. What would it mean to think of tears not as the useless by-product of a too-full heart but as a disruption? Expressing a feeling publicly, visibly, can be a surprising move, a powerful intervention. When a person cries in public—on the bus, say—a space for connection opens up that wasn't there before. Maybe a stranger offers a bottle of water or a tissue; maybe another stranger asks, quietly, if the crier is all right. Maybe someone sits down and offers to listen. It's just as likely, of course, that none of this happens at all: a person cries on the bus and everyone moves silently around them, embarrassed, pretending not to see. But the important truth is that they *do* see, and they're reminded that human feeling is alive and real, all around them, all the time.

WHEN A PERSON CRIES AT work, that, too, is a Pisces act of asserting their humanity, and the enduring humanity of everyone around them. Because the magical thing about crying at work is the ripples of feeling that emanate outward from the crier, affecting everyone else in the room, too. Everyone's attention is drawn away, at least for a second, from their work and back to their shared, soft, emotional humanity.

When I worked in a kitchen—the same one managed by the man who scorned Mariah Carey's so-called vocal Olympics—my coworker and friend had her heart broken by a man. The heartbreak was brutal, a skidding, bumping, slow-burn kind of drama—the kind of breakup that seemed, every time, as though it might not be final, as though real love might still be possible. And every time, of course, the possibility of love kept getting pushed out of reach.

Over the weeks that this breakup happened, my friend would periodically retreat during her shift to the back corner of the kitchen, between the industrial fridge and the dishwashing station, to sit down on a milk crate and quietly cry. As for us—the rest of the kitchen staff, the baristas up front, and even the booksellers who worked next door—we were concerned for our friend. So the pastry chef would bring her a macaron from the case, or the butcher would fry up a scrap of leftover sausage for her, or whoever was playing the music would put on a song we knew she liked. The manager, of course, hated this, wishing we would please deal with tomorrow's prep work, please wipe down the counters, please return quickly to our roles as workers.

But for all of us, even for the manager, tears were a reminder of our shared humanity. The tears distracted us; they took us away from our tasks; they reminded us that we were people first, with feelings that could not be conveniently compartmentalized or defanged or hidden away, no matter how much any boss tried to make it so. They reminded us that we were, above all else, *people*, and our primary responsibility was never to our kitchen tasks but to each other.

In the end, even when Pisces energy *is* all about the tears, that doesn't mean it's weak. There's a rebelliousness there, too. Living with so much feeling, after all, requires enormous amounts of courage. It's simple and satisfying to imagine that Pisces emotion is steady and unchanging, like sinking into a soft pillow. But emotion can disturb the universe, and disturbing the universe requires bravery and will. "I think that will is the great unseen and unacknowledged ingredient in Fred's story," journalist Tom Junod said in the Rogers documentary. It might be the great unacknowledged ingredient in Pisces as well. It takes an incredible amount of sheer will, after all, to remain so soft in this world.

THERE'S ONE STORY FROM THE Wayside School books that shows more than any other what a Pisces energy can be about. This one is from *Wayside School Is Falling Down*, and it concerns a student named Calvin, whose birthday it is. Because he's constantly losing his toys, he tells his classmates, his parents have agreed to get him something he'll never lose this year: a tattoo. The appointment is booked; Calvin just needs to decide what he wants to get. Stephen suggests a snake, Deedee an eagle, Kathy a dead rat, Jason a naked woman. Calvin isn't sure. How can he know what he'll want for the rest of his life? He thinks he's decided to get a snake fighting a leopard, but when the appointment time actually arrives, he changes his mind. The violent image of a snake and leopard fighting, on his body, forever? No. Louis Sachar, a Pisces, gives this character a moment of gentle Piscean grace instead. On his ankle, Calvin gets a tattoo of a potato. When he returns to school, his classmates all make fun of it: it's so silly, so soft. Calvin, though, knows his feelings, and he knows what will make him happy. And after the story ends, as he gets older, the potato will be there to remind him that his feelings mattered when he was a child and that they'll continue mattering no matter how grown up he gets.

Conclusion

FTER THE SUN FINISHES TRAVELING THROUGH PISCES, IT ENTERS ARIES AGAIN, AND PISCES, WHOSE WISDOM IS SO COMPLETE AS TO SEEM ALMOST CHILDLIKE, GIVES WAY ONCE MORE TO ARIES'S CHILDLIKE EXUBERANCE. The days will begin to grow longer and the sky bluer, and whether it's Aries's fire sign energy or simply the changing seasons of the natural world, life might begin to feel exhilarating again, your body might begin to feel powerful again, and everything that seemed impossible might become straightforward once more. Like so many things in the natural world, astrology moves cyclically, offering second chances to live the way you want—second chances to see the world clearly, and to step ever more fully into your power.

As a system, astrology relies on movement and connection. The planets never stop moving, and neither do our lives here on earth. The signs aren't arbitrary lists of traits, but twelve delicately balanced, interconnected parts of a whole. If any one of the signs were to be somehow removed from the cycle, the entire system would lose cohesion. Each sign reacts to and builds on the sign before it, inheriting part of the previous sign's wisdom and attempting to address part of the previous sign's weakness. The signs need each other to make sense, just as we need each other to know ourselves. There's no way to see ourselves clearly in isolation.

This means that astrology can't offer you an unchanging image of a self in stasis. It can't offer you certainty, or a narrative of linear progress, or knowledge of the future. It can't offer you an exemption from the difficult work of growing up, of learning to love yourself. Rather, it can give you tools to learn, to try, to become slowly wiser and more generous. It can teach you to fight for the beauty, or the freedom, or the nurturing love you really need. Astrology can remind you of all the incredible ways you can be soft, and the incredible ways you can be brave.

With any luck, by the end of this book you'll have seen something true of yourself. And with any luck, you'll have seen some things you disagree with, too. Some disagreement is, in the end, a good thing; astrologers exist in a state of constant disagreement with one another. There is no certainty here, and no final authority. There's no one here to enforce the rules or tell you who you really are. Astrology can gesture toward meaning, but in the end it's up to you to learn how to see yourself and decide how to live.

Astrology won't give you some kind of perfect, unwavering certainty about yourself and your life. What it does have to give is so much better: a rich sense of connection with the world, and an understanding of your own place in it. You're only one person in the world; you don't need to be everything, only you. And to do that, you're already exactly where you need to be.

Acknowledgments

Thank you to my editor, Sarah Haugen, for understanding the soul of this project, and the rest of the team at Harper: Katherine Beitner, Kristin Cipolla, Nate Knaebel, Sarah Lambert, Joanne O'Neill, and Bonni Leon-Berman. Thank you to my agent, Dana Murphy, for guiding me into the weird world of book publishing, and for believing in me and making it count.

Thank you to my smart and generous editors at The Cut: Callie Beusman, Jen Gann, and Molly Fischer.

Thank you to the Loft Literary Center, especially Kathryn Savage, and the writers of the 2017–2018 Mentor Series, especially Karen Gu, Victoria Blanco, and Nneka Onwuzurike. Thank you to the writers of Grace Paley Palooza, especially Emma Eisenberg and Sarah Marshall.

Thank you to the Saint Paul Public Library and the Freelance Solidarity Project.

Thank you to the people whose support had nothing directly to do with writing or astrology, and everything to do with helping me grow and making it bearable, even joyful, to live in this world. Thanks especially to: Andrea Rissing, without whose friendship I'd be utterly lost. Anney Traymany, whose sharp, clear mind makes mine sharper. Ben Linder, a beacon of goodness and integrity since we were the littlest preteens. Eleanor Russell, whose independent Aquarian brilliance I trust completely. Kye Ginger, who has shown me, over and over again, the very best of loyal Gemini love. Mina Seck, whose generous kindness brought me back to life. Rosie Jacobson, who completely gets it and who's loved me through the worst bad days. Sarah Zidonik, endlessly caring and endlessly fun, who has been there for me in more ways than I could ever list. Shomari M. Harris, the best mentor and wisest friend a person could hope to have.

Thank you to my first editor and brilliant friend Molly McArdle, without whom this book—and all the writing I've ever done about astrology—would not exist, and Jen May, an unsung genius whose visual language has shaped so much.

Thank you to Soleil Ho, the best there is, forever and ever and ever and ever.

Thank you to Dave Embree, without whose encouragement and support this book would not have been written, and who is, as that tearful mom once said on *The Bachelor*, my angel.

Thank you to all my family, especially my cousins Katie Kitson and Julia Gay. Thank you most of all to Abby Comstock-Gay Güner, Hannah Comstock-Gay, Lucy Comstock-Gay, and Stuart Comstock-Gay, whose love and support has made everything possible.

About the Author

CLAIRE COMSTOCK-GAY is a writer and astrologer whose weekly horoscopes appear on *New York* magazine's The Cut. She has written for the *New York Times* and has been featured on NPR's *On Point* and *Bitch* magazine's *Popaganda* podcast. She lives in Minneapolis, Minnesota.